LAST BELL

LAST BELL

Breaking the gridlock in education reform

Carl Bistany *and* Stephanie Gruner Buckley

P

PROFILE BOOKS

First published in Great Britain in 2015 by
Profile Books Ltd
3 Holford Yard
Bevin Way
London WC1X 9HD
www.profilebooks.com

1 3 5 7 9 10 8 6 4 2

The right of Carl Bistany and Stephanie Gruner Buckley to
be identified as the authors of this work has been asserted in
accordance with the Copyright, Designs and Patents Act 1988.

A CIP catalogue record for this book is available from The British Library

ISBN 978 1 78125 630 5
eISBN 978 1 78283 244 7

All reasonable efforts have been made to obtain copyright permissions where
required. Any omissions and errors of attribution are unintentional and
will, if notified in writing to the publisher, be corrected in future printings.

Designed by sue@lambledesign.demon.co.uk
Typeset in Photina by MacGuru Ltd
info@macguru.org.uk

Printed and bound in Italy by L.E.G.O. S.p.A.

FSC
www.fsc.org
MIX
Paper from
responsible sources
FSC® C023419

Because our children deserve better

Contents

Figures, photos, and tables

Foreword

THE UNITED STATES is the wealthiest nation in the world. Two factors are generally mentioned as critical to this success: A set of economic institutions that promote efficient and innovative markets and an historical record of broad investment in the human capital of its people. By maintaining generally free and open labor and capital markets, workers and firms adapt quickly to the changing demands for different goods and services. And, particularly as seen from my office in the middle of Silicon Valley, there is fierce competition for highly skilled workers. The result is an innovative and dynamic economy that is the envy of the world.

The stark contrast between the vibrant U.S. economy and the stagnant and expensive U.S. K-12 public school system is, then, difficult for many to reconcile. How can most of the economy thrive while its public schools do not? It surely cannot be a lack of appreciation for education, because nobody doubts the importance of quality education.

Economists have less difficulty than many in reconciling this dichotomy. The private economy provides clear incentives to participants—workers, firms, and consumers. Skilled workers are matched with good jobs. Firms that provide products that consumers want, and do so at competitive prices, grow and survive. Consumers make choices in their purchases, and these choices—and the ensuing competition among firms—drive firms to innovate, to provide goods at reasonable prices, and to ensure that the quality of goods satisfies consumers. And this all happens with firms making profits—or disappearing from the market in the fashion of American Motors, Blockbuster, Borders, Pan American World Airways, and Woolworth's, when they do not.

Stacked against the thriving private economy are the sheltered nonmarket operations of U.S. public schools, lacking the incentives that are commonplace elsewhere. In the public school sector, "incentives" and "competition" are bad words— but not nearly as bad as "for-profit." It is possible to have entire conversations at a philosophical level about the dangers of for-profit firms in public education without ever touching on student outcomes or efficiency, subjects that one might think to be at the heart of the discussion. It is more a pseudo-moral argument about whether anyone should make a profit in providing something as important as education.

This brings us to *Last Bell: Breaking the gridlock in education reform.* There is a simple storyline: Energetic, worldwide firm (SABIS) meets the largely immovable object of publicly run schools in the U.S. They bring a real track record of performance, and yet they repeatedly face obstacles that would be unacceptable in other sectors.

The compelling part of this book is the firsthand experience with public school officials and decision makers, both elected and appointed, who fight competition, particularly from for-profit providers, at every turn. It is useful to put some of the recurring arguments they make against for-profit involvement into perspective.

Perhaps the most repeated argument, one that has the

tone of being finely honed at a set of focus groups, is that for-profit providers running public charter schools would provide a shoddy product that is priced too high (presumably because there is a layer of profit being skimmed off the top). What is most surprising about this argument is the low level of regard expressed for the parents. All discussions of choice in education are just that—providing choice, particularly where little exists today. If it is a shoddy product, the parents do not have to choose it, and implicitly the firm providing the bad education cannot make a profit and will fail to survive. Nobody makes such a foolish argument in the 80 percent of the U.S. economy involving private, for-profit firms. The image that is evoked by this argument is that of East Germans stubbornly sticking to their Trabants after the Berlin Wall came down instead of doing the obvious, which was immediately driving their Trabants into the West, abandoning them, and buying Volkswagens. Parents, like their East German counterparts released from government-run monopolies, should have an opportunity to make choices, and the waiting lists for good charter schools show their ability to make choices.

Of course, this discussion also points to an underlying inequity in the provision of public education in the U.S. Middle-income parents regularly exercise school choice—not, in general, by selecting a charter or a private school, but by choosing a residence in the school district of their choice. It is low-income parents who typically lack choice, particularly when they live in school districts without good education options and cannot afford to move.

Again, it is instructive to follow the clear discussion of the obstacles to providing educational choice that Carl Bistany and Stephanie Gruner Buckley set out. The arguments opponents make against choice are scattered in all directions: Our schools are doing fine so we don't need anything more; teachers are over-burdened by increasing numbers of poor kids and it's not the fault of the schools; for-profit schools are not accountable to the public.

These are the arguments of those who are most concerned with maintaining the current schools just as they are, and empirical support for their arguments is irrelevant as long as people accept them without thinking too deeply. This status quo motivation is most clearly seen by the oft-repeated accusation that a major problem with charter schools is that they take money away from the traditional public schools, money that clearly is necessary because the poor student results show the obvious need. Notwithstanding the fact that with less money they also have fewer students to educate, this has the ring of "If you don't force people to buy Trabants, there might be less demand and thus fewer workers employed in Trabant factories."

Perhaps the most interesting argument is one that puts the issue in complete perspective: Our schools must be fine because we have such a strong economy. That is the heart of the matter. We have managed to outpace other economies by having very strong economic institutions traditionally fed by people with more schooling than found anyplace else in the world. But these advantages are disappearing. We have a lower high school graduation rate than all but six OECD countries, and this ranking matches the quality ranking on international math and science tests. In the future, as more countries adopt our economic institutions, we will have to compete on the skills of our population—where we have slipped badly.

The main theme of this book is simple. Attracting people

who know how to run high-quality schools, whether they come from for-profit firms or not, must be a high priority. We owe it to our children and to the nation. We particularly owe it to disadvantaged children who are not getting the skills necessary to compete in today's knowledge-based economy.

Eric A. Hanushek
Stanford, California
July 2015

Introduction

IN THE MID-1990s, a private education provider offered to take over the worst performing public elementary school in one of America's most violent cities.[1] The education provider was SABIS®,[2] and the school was the William N. DeBerry Elementary School in Springfield, Massachusetts. Not far from the school were boarded up houses and people selling drugs on the street in broad daylight. Student achievement at DeBerry was the lowest in the district. The school needed a complete overhaul. Yet DeBerry parents and teachers, convinced that SABIS, a for-profit organization, cared more for profits than children, said "no." Undeterred, the education provider offered to take over the next worst performing elementary school in the district.

The city's school superintendent at the time, Peter Negroni, suggested the Alfred Glickman School. This elementary school was located in a predominantly white, middle-class neighborhood in Springfield, but because of a racial busing policy, two-thirds of the school's students were minorities, and 80 percent (more than double the state average)[3] were eligible for federal lunch subsidies.[4] Academic and discipline problems were common. Parents and local officials, by a narrow margin, approved the move and a charter was eventually awarded to SABIS.

That was two decades ago. Today, the school (renamed the SABIS® International Charter School, or SICS, and expanded to grade 12) is a six-time silver medalist in *U.S. News & World Report*'s annual "America's Best High Schools" listing.[5] Parents of kids at the school think it is pretty good too. Every graduate of the school for more than a decade has been offered a two- or four-year college place, including at Ivy League universities such as Columbia, Yale, and Harvard. It is not surprising that there are some 3,000 kids on the school's waiting list.

Over at the DeBerry School, things haven't changed much in twenty years. The school remains among the worst performing elementary schools in the district and, indeed, the state.[6] In 2012, the Massachusetts Department of Elementary and Secondary Education named DeBerry a Level 4 school,[7] which means it is seriously struggling and requires extraordinary measures to turn it around. Stefania Raschilla, one of the district's star principals, has been brought in and given three years to fix things. If she fails, the school will, in all likelihood, go into receivership and the entire staff could be forced out.

The DeBerry School is not unique, nor sadly was the negative response from parents and teachers when offered a chance to start afresh. I appreciate, however, that emotions run high when it comes to public education. People are loyal to their local teachers and principals, and, as a result, sometimes make bad choices. The trouble is that bad choices are being made on a much larger scale too.

Billions of taxpayer dollars and charitable donations are spent annually trying to fix failing public schools, particularly in poor communities, but progress has been slow and incremental at best. This has been going on for more than three decades, yet one obvious solution—turning to the free market and for-profit companies like SABIS to help build more competitive schools—is still greeted with fear and hostility. Why?

This is the question my book sets out to answer: Why is America failing to embrace a free market strategy for public education when so many students and schools would clearly benefit?

As it stands, for-profit education management companies are allowed to run public schools (otherwise known as charter schools or public charter schools) in most states, but can compete only on a hugely uneven playing field. That is because those opposed to any kind of private sector involvement have done everything in their power to create major obstacles, making the mission of turning around derelict schools much more difficult.

These obstacles include reduced public funding per pupil and limited, if any, funding for facilities; unrealistically short contracts, which make it difficult for education management organizations to raise financing; opaque authorization and renewal processes; and legislative bans in some states that make it illegal for for-profits to operate at all.

When charters for public schools are granted in a state, there is no guarantee of renewing the charter or even keeping it for the full life of the charter, even when the school is meeting—if not exceeding—its goals.

The stability of schools, teachers' jobs, and students' education in America is regularly undermined by arbitrary decisions made by some state legislatures. Here is one example. In 2010, SABIS ran a school in Georgia for nearly nine months before local districts successfully appealed to the state's Supreme Court, claiming that our charter (as well as other charters in the state) was unconstitutional. The charters in question had been awarded legally by a state entity, yet district officials felt that they should have sole authorizing power to issue charters for all public schools. Even though a lower court disagreed with the district officials and had given authority to the state body, the higher court sided with the districts, resulting in the forced closure of our school and others.

Two years later, a constitutional amendment restored authorizing power to the state. Sadly, it was too late for our school, and it cost us dearly—not to mention what it cost our students. We had spent hundreds of thousands of dollars in startup costs to hire teachers and suppliers, buy equipment, and secure a lease, and then paid even more for temporary accommodation for nearly 600 students for three months when refurbishments on the main building were delayed due to more red tape. There were only losses from this endeavor as we had deferred management fees during the startup phase. The school needed the cash for more important things, like getting up and running. Then, after nearly nine months of operating the school, the charter was revoked. With all of these obstacles, it is no wonder so few for-profit companies run charter schools. It is just too risky.

There is a lot of hysteria surrounding for-profit participation in public schools and many misconceptions. The media is filled with polarizing, unproductive talk from those on both sides of the debate. At one extreme are those who argue that the U.S. is doomed economically and socially without a complete overhaul of the public education system. They say that those opposed to school choice (meaning alternative public school options such as charter schools) are like socialists who fear a market economy, and that their so-called democratic ideals are strangling public schools. On the other side are school choice's most ardent critics, who claim that public education does not even need saving. They accuse those who say it does of participating in a mass conspiracy to dismantle the public school system and get rich at the expense of the nation's children. They warn that schools must be protected from these profiteers whose goal is to replace public education with unregulated, unsupervised, and unaccountable schools—all on the taxpayers' dime. Lost in the debate are the needs of the children.

This hyperbole is not helpful, nor is it accurate, yet many lawmakers are listening. Even as I write, legislators across the country are discussing how to curb charter school growth, reduce funding, or eliminate for-profit education providers altogether.

From the very beginning of the charter school movement, reform progress has been stymied at every turn by people with vested interests in preserving the status quo, including leaders of teachers unions, school district officials, and obliging lawmakers who push measures to undermine for-profit participation and, really, all charter school expansion. As a result, more than twenty years after the first charter school appeared, the nation still lacks a competitive market for public education, is falling behind other nations academically, and is producing too few high school graduates who are ready for college— much less prepared for jobs in a fast-paced global economy.

So where do I fit into all of this? I am the president of the board of SABIS, the same education provider that turned a failing school in Springfield into a six-time silver medalist in *U.S. News and World Report*'s "Best High Schools in America" report. I am the fourth-generation leader of an education business that is run by two families and was set up in 1886 in a village in Lebanon. For 22 years, I have helped guide our expansion, particularly through public–private partnerships, so that today SABIS® Network schools operate in 16 countries on four continents (Asia, Africa, Europe, and North America). Fifteen of our schools with more than 9,000 students are in the U.S.

Helping me to explore this topic is Stephanie Gruner Buckley, a longtime journalist, who has worked on staff at publications including *The Wall Street Journal, Inc.* magazine and Atlantic Media's *Quartz*. We wrote the book in the first person to make it more accessible to readers and to reflect my strongly held views, but it truly was a joint effort. What started for Stephanie as little more than an interesting reporting and writing assignment has turned into something far more meaningful. I daresay that after a year spent investigating the issues surrounding charter school reform, she feels as passionately as I do about getting this message out.

Now, I would like to share with you my main message and explain what this book is about. First, I am for raising education standards and for genuinely making this a national priority. People have been saying this for decades, but without seeing significant change. Yes, there are many excellent schools in the U.S., with graduation rates at historic highs, but standards must be raised for everyone, particularly for the kids most in need—those from the nation's poorest families, minorities, and English learners in urban and rural areas. Traditional public schools are failing so many of these children and all while the U.S. spends 39 percent more per pupil than does the average industrialized nation.[8]

I believe people agree more than they disagree about the need for education reform, but politics, special interests, and emotions have muddied the waters and made it difficult to find a way forward. Clearly, we all agree that what matters most is the children and making sure that all of them are prepared for the future.

I believe that raising education standards requires a bipartisan approach, and that parents, not politicians or union officials, should decide where to send their children to school. I believe that parents of students at failing schools should have other options.

And yes, I believe in a free market. I think the best way to prepare all children in the U.S. for a bright future is by opening up education to those organizations that can offer the best results, as has been done in other social sectors such as healthcare, transportation, and infrastructure.

Specifically, I am referring to for-profit companies like SABIS. I believe that the country's public education sector will not succeed without the involvement of for-profit companies. But just because I believe in a free market does not mean I believe in an unregulated market. I think that all education providers—whether for-profit or not—must be held accountable.

There is a lot of misunderstanding about the accountability of for-profit companies that run public schools, and also about their profits. Let me explain briefly how charter schools work, make money, and are held accountable. (I return to this subject in detail later in the book.) While states vary, in general an education provider is employed to manage a school for a fee by an independent, nonprofit board of trustees made up of local citizens—typically ones who care about education. In our U.S. charter model, the board approves the operating budget, and if there is a profit, it remains on the board's accounts.[9]

The board's members decide what to do with that profit—whether to spend it on improvements to the school building or make bond financing payments if the purchase of a facility was involved, or to expand an art or music program. A profit is a good thing, as it reflects efficient management and means that more money can be invested in the school.

Charter schools are held accountable for their use of funds through an audit process. These public schools are audited by an independent public accountant who issues financial statements, which are then made public and submitted to the authorizers (the official bodies that award school charters). Schools must report how every dime is spent.[10] In this way, taxpayer money is protected. There are penalties for companies that misrepresent the numbers; when this happens, they are prosecuted.

Are there charlatans who abuse the system? Of course. There are bad actors everywhere, including in public schools. But this does not mean the good actors should be eliminated. Here I would like to make something clear. I am not out to get rid of good traditional public schools; it is the failing ones that I am talking about. Here parents need options.

The aim of this book is to reduce the fear and hyperbole in this debate. It is also to give decision makers the facts about the role for-profits play in public education and to chart a way forward that puts first the interests of America's children. I speak with a sense of urgency. Education is critical to a nation's social and economic wellbeing, and the time to reform it is now. A last bell is sounding for public education in America, and we must answer it.

CHAPTER 1

America's future: failing grades and falling behind

RAISING EDUCATION STANDARDS has been a national priority for more than thirty years. Ever since the 1983 government publication of *A Nation at Risk*, which argued that the dramatic decline of public education threatened the nation,[1] education reform has been hotly debated and a key part of local, state, and federal agendas. Yet despite some progress over three decades and a lot of tinkering, the state of many American public schools and the performance of students remain causes for alarm.

Instead of alarm, those opposed to school choice and free market involvement continue to applaud the system, even when faced with clear evidence of its failings. In October 2014, during a visit to one of Michigan's worst performing public schools, Lily Eskelsen García, president of the National Education Association (NEA) union, told staff that theirs was "a school that did it right."[2] The school at the time was among the lowest performing 6 percent of public schools in the state. It hardly qualified for any sort of praise.

Many people like to suggest that across the nation students are doing just fine. They go as far as saying that an authoritative, nationwide assessment of students' reading and math skills by the National Assessment of Education Progress (NAEP), otherwise known as the "Nation's Report Card," indicates that the U.S. does not even have a problem because there has been progress over the past two decades.

They are right, to a degree. There has been progress over time, depending on where you look. But what they fail to say is that a startling percentage of kids are being let down by the public education system. The NAEP assessment released in May 2014 shows that a quarter of U.S. high school seniors lack basic reading skills, while 35 percent lack basic math skills.[3] These numbers have not improved much over the years. On the contrary, reading performance for 12th-graders has worsened since 1992.[4] And since the previous review in 2009, achievement scores have stalled in both subjects.

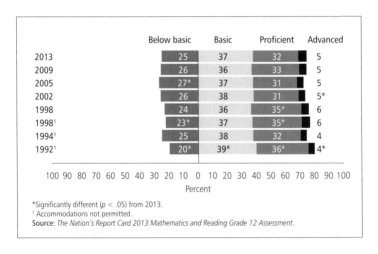

Figure 1.1 NAEP reading results for 12th-graders over time[5]

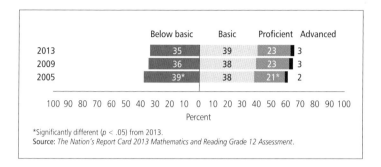

Figure 1.2 NAEP math results for 12th-graders over time[6]

Faced with these dismal results, people who support staying the course argue that the NAEP numbers are misleading and that the standards regarding what a student should know on this assessment are subjective. While I would agree that no national student assessment is perfect, it is hard to ignore the bottom line: Results from the 2014 "Nation's Report Card" show that as many as one in four American high school seniors may be functionally illiterate,[7,8] suggesting an inability to read or write well enough to perform basic, everyday tasks like filling out a job application or reading a medicine bottle.

Roughly one in three American high school seniors would earn a D or below in math,[9] meaning many of them could be entering adulthood without the ability to easily calculate their change at a supermarket checkout counter. No one, not even the biggest cheerleaders of the current public education system, is happy with the high percentage of high school students performing below this basic level.

The picture is even more alarming if you look at the latest NAEP math and reading results for minority students. Yes, black students have shown progress over time, but black 12th-graders tested in 2013 were still about 2.5 times more likely than white 12th-graders to perform below the basic level in reading and math, according to the Education Trust, a charity that promotes high academic achievement, particularly for low-income and minority students.[10] Hispanic, American Indian, and Alaska Native students were about twice as likely as white students to perform below the basic level in these subjects, added the organization, while only about one in ten low-income students performed at or above a proficient level in math.[11]

Performance gaps between different races and ethnicities have not changed much in reading or math since 2009, according to NAEP, and indeed the gap in reading between white and black students widened from 1992 to 2013.[12]

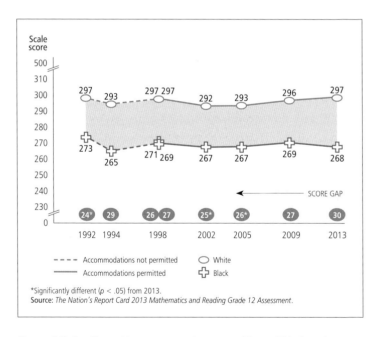

Figure 1.3 Reading achievement gaps between white and black students over time[13]

Not surprisingly, life after high school is more difficult for the average minority student than it is for the average white student—and the problem has gotten worse in recent years. The gap between black and white students, as well as between Hispanic and white students, who earned a bachelor's degree or higher expanded significantly between 1990 and 2013, according to a report from the National Center for Education Statistics.[14]

> *In 2013, some 34 percent of 25- to 29-year-olds had earned a bachelor's or higher degree. Between 1990 and 2013, the size of the White–Black gap at this education level widened from 13 to 20 percentage points, and the White–Hispanic gap widened from 18 to 25 percentage points.*[15]

Chronic achievement gaps have serious consequences. A study by the World Bank shows that, on average, each year of schooling raises an individual's earning potential by more than 10 percent a year.[16] Wealth inequality in America has become a big issue, and while there are many causes, chronic education achievement gaps cannot help. More alarming still, these wealth gaps are growing along racial and ethnic lines. According to the Pew Research Center, wealth inequality in the U.S. has widened significantly since 1983, with white adults typically faring far better financially than black and Hispanic adults.[17] (See Figure 1.4 on page 14.)

The other figure often cited by public education champions as a sign that all is well is the annual high school graduation rate, the most recent of which showed that 80 percent of students completed high school in four years and received a regular high school diploma for the school year 2011–12.[18] Clearly, it is good news that nearly four out of five students

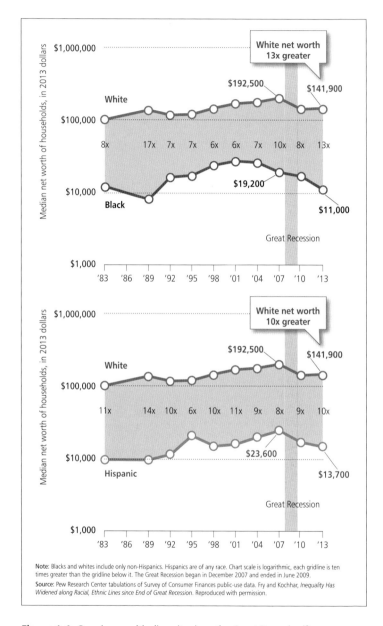

Figure 1.4 Growing wealth disparity since the Great Recession[19]

received a regular high school diploma within four years of starting the ninth grade for the first time. The trouble comes when you break down the numbers by ethnic group and socio-economic status.

While white students enjoyed a graduation rate of 86 percent, which was above the national average, black and Hispanic students scored far below the national average at 69 percent and 73 percent, respectively.[20] Economically disadvantaged students had a four-year graduation rate of 72 percent, while students with limited English proficiency came in at 59 percent.[21]

What of those young people who did not graduate in four years with a regular diploma? U.S. Education Secretary Arne Duncan said in 2014 that the 20 percent represents 718,000 young people, among them a sharply disproportionate share of African Americans, Hispanics, Native Americans, and students from low-income families. He added that those students without high school diplomas face lives of "poverty and misery."[22]

Soon after the graduation numbers came out in 2014, Robert Balfanz, a research professor at Johns Hopkins University School of Education, wrote an editorial for the *New York Times*, in which he said that while more than three million students would receive a high school diploma in 2014, one-third of the nation's black and Hispanic young men would not.[23] "In an era when there is virtually no legal work for dropouts, these young men face a bleak future," he wrote.[24]

Figure 1.5 on the following page is a good indicator of what failing to have a degree likely means.[25]

Another chart from Balfanz's "Building a Grad Nation" report, an "annual update on America's high school dropout crisis," shows graduation rates of black, Hispanic, and white

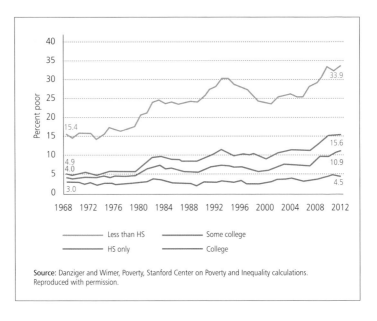

Percent poor

40
35
30 .... 33.9
25
20
15.4 15
15.6
10
4.9
4.0 5 10.9
3.0 0 4.5

1968 1972 1976 1980 1984 1988 1992 1996 2000 2004 2008 2012

——— Less than HS ——— Some college
——— HS only ——— College

Source: Danziger and Wimer, Poverty, Stanford Center on Poverty and Inequality calculations.
Reproduced with permission.

Figure 1.5 Poverty rates by educational attainment, persons aged 25–64

students. While it is indeed good news that graduation rates are improving, the gaps between student groups have not altered much over the years. (See Figure 1.6 opposite.)

Here I would like to point out that it is not just minority and low-income students that the public education system is letting down. The majority of students—minority, low-income, or otherwise—who go on to college find that they are ill-prepared for the academic challenges they face there. In 2014, the National Center for Education Statistics, which linked NAEP results with college preparedness, said that just 39 percent of 12th-graders possessed the necessary math skills for entry-level college coursework, while only 38 percent had the required reading skills.[26] As it stands, at least a fifth of college freshmen need to take noncredit, remedial classes.[27]

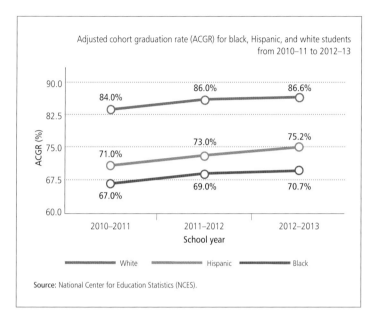

Figure 1.6 Graduation rates by races[28]

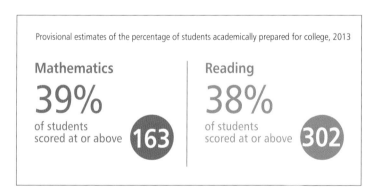

Figure 1.7 Percentage of students who are ready for college[29]

Upon release of these figures, David Driscoll, chair of the National Assessment Governing Board, which oversees and sets policy for NAEP, said: "Our job is to be the gold standard, the truth-teller. But clearly this is not acceptable, so I'm hoping people will get energized about this."[30]

It is indeed time to get energized. The U.S. is falling behind other nations academically. American 15-year-olds do not even rank in the top 20 of the world's most developed countries in overall reading, math, and science scores, according to the Program for International Student Assessment (PISA), which measures the scholastic performance of 15-year-olds around the world.[31] American students score below average in math compared to students in the world's most developed countries and rank only about average in science and reading.[32] Over the past decade, U.S. students have shown little, if any, progress in reading, math, and science scores.[33]

Of greater concern, however, is that American students are falling further and further behind, with an increasing number of countries outperforming the U.S. in math, science, and reading.[34] In 2012, 29 nations and jurisdictions surpassed the U.S. in math, up from 23 three years ago. In science, students from 22 nations scored better than the U.S. student average, up from 18 in 2009.[35] In reading, 19 nations outperformed the U.S., up from 9 in 2009. Overall, the U.S. ranked two places behind Russia, falling between the Slovak Republic and Lithuania.[36] A key question is whether the U.S. public education system is adequately preparing young people to compete in global markets. Sadly, the numbers suggest it is not. Education Secretary Duncan said the findings showed a "picture of educational stagnation,"[37] while Harvard Business School professor Jan Rivkin said:

> Other countries that were behind us, like Italy and Portugal, are now catching up. We are in a race in the global economy.

The problem is not that we're slowing down. The problem is that the other runners are getting faster.[38]

The failure to significantly improve public education and to provide equal access to high quality education threatens the long-term competitiveness of the U.S. economy. My father, Ralph Bistany, one of SABIS's third-generation leaders, recalls how in the late 1940s if you wanted a decent car, you would buy an American one. Why was that? Because the U.S. had more and better trained engineers than any other country. He did not think that would ever change.

If you had asked me then, what's the future of cars, I would say there's no way any other country can compete. The Americans have such an advantage. Nobody can catch up with them. But no more. They are no longer producing enough scientists and engineers.

The reality is that too few American high school graduates (partly because they are unprepared), go into the STEM (science, technology, engineering, and math) fields in college. Instead, the best graduate science and engineering schools in the U.S. are filled with foreigners. Of the roughly 38,000 doctorates in science and engineering awarded by U.S. universities in 2011, foreign students on temporary visas earned 56 percent of the engineering doctorates, 51 percent of all computer sciences doctorates, 44 percent of physics doctorates, and 60 percent of economics doctorates.[39] Overall, non-U.S. citizens earned about one-third of all science and engineering degrees, according to this 2014 U.S. government report on higher education in science and engineering from the National Science Foundation.[40]

So, what happens when all of those foreign engineers,

computer scientists, physicists, and economists take their degrees and go home? *New York Times* columnist Thomas Friedman wrote back in 2009:

> *... we should be stapling a green card to the diploma of any foreign student who earns an advanced degree at any U.S. university, and we should be ending all H-1B visa restrictions on knowledge workers who want to come here. They would invent many more jobs than they would supplant. The world's best brains are on sale. Let's buy more!*[41]

Six years on, that is not what is happening. U.S. immigration policies still make it challenging to keep foreign students in America after graduation. They can stay temporarily, thanks to the Optional Practical Training (OPT) program, but the path to permanent residency remains long and arduous.

There was a time when foreign graduates would jump through hoops to stay in the U.S., but today, that is less and less the case. For many of these graduates there are better opportunities back home, as a high percentage of them come from large countries with fast-growing economies such as China and India.[42]

The U.S. already has a serious skills shortage in these highly technical areas. Just ask any high-tech employer in America how easy it is to fill a job. The situation is so bad that Microsoft leaders in 2014 announced they would open a training and development center in Vancouver, British Columbia, instead of back home in the U.S. While tax breaks probably had something to do with the move, a Microsoft executive said that the public should expect more decisions like this as long as Congress fails to raise the cap on H-1B visas, which allow U.S. companies to employ foreigners in specialty fields.[43]

Where does all this leave things? Ultimately, what is at stake is the fate of a nation. This is no exaggeration. There are serious social and economic consequences that result from declining education standards. Also of major concern is the fact that America's most disadvantaged youth are increasingly losing out.

Over the past three decades, as officials have tinkered with public education—sometimes making things better, sometimes not—the achievement gap between high- and low-income students has widened by some 40 percent, according to a study by the Stanford Center on Poverty and Inequality.[44] There are a lot of reasons for this widening gap, and they could be debated for another three decades, but America cannot afford to wait.

In 2015, the U.S. crossed a shocking threshold as new statistics showed that more than half of students at public schools were living in poverty.[45, 46] This means we are no longer talking about declining standards for a disadvantaged few, but rather declining standards for a majority of public school students whose success or failure at school will determine the nation's future.

Already things look bleak. The same 2014 Stanford report, which highlighted the widening gap between high- and low-income students, called the period under review among the "very worst" of any covered since 2000.[47, 48] Just about every indicator in this report, including poverty rates, employment numbers, income gaps, and disparities in education, health, and wealth, presents a "broadly deteriorating poverty and inequality landscape," the authors concluded. "The facts of the matter, when laid out so starkly," they wrote, "are quite overwhelming."[49] The report ends with a section on education and a final thought that the situation is unlikely to change "without focused policy attention on improving both our schools and the wide economic disparities that inhibit the educational success of the nation's children."[50]

A nation's promise

All, regardless of race or class or economic status, are entitled to a fair chance and to the tools for developing their individual powers of mind and spirit to the utmost. This promise means that all children by virtue of their own efforts, competently guided, can hope to attain the mature and informed judgment needed to secure gainful employment, and to manage their own lives, thereby serving not only their own interests but also the progress of society itself.

Source: *A Nation at Risk,* 1983[51]

Few people dispute the need to boost academic achievement across the country; it is how best to accomplish this that stirs up controversy. So now, I would like to discuss what has been tried over the past three decades and look at what has and has not worked.

America has tried spending more money, but that has not made much difference. Between 1970 and 2009, government at all levels nearly tripled its spending to an average of $149,000 on the 13-year education of a high school senior.[52] In total, the U.S. spends more than $550 billion a year on public elementary and secondary education,[53] while federal spending alone is nearly $79 billion annually on primary and secondary education programs.[54]

Yet, while the U.S. spends more per student than most other countries, this does not translate into better academic performance. Harvard's Jan Rivkin points out that the Slovak Republic spends about $53,000 per student and performs at the same level as the U.S.[55]

Spending more and more money is not the answer. Just take a look at Figure 1.8 from a Cato Institute report, analyzing increased public school spending and the academic performance of 17-year-old public school students over time.[56]

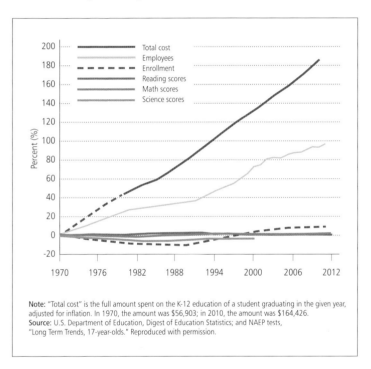

Note: "Total cost" is the full amount spent on the K-12 education of a student graduating in the given year, adjusted for inflation. In 1970, the amount was $56,903; in 2010, the amount was $164,426.
Source: U.S. Department of Education, Digest of Education Statistics; and NAEP tests, "Long Term Trends, 17-year-olds." Reproduced with permission.

Figure 1.8 Trends in American public schooling since 1970

Wealthy Americans have thrown billions of dollars at the education problem without generating substantial returns or sustainable results. Facebook's Mark Zuckerberg pledged $100 million in 2010[57] to the Newark school district in the hope of rescuing it. He did not rescue it, and so far the funds have had little impact on student achievement, while millions of dollars have gone to consultants.[58] Then there is the Bill & Melinda Gates Foundation, which spent more than a billion dollars alone analyzing whether smaller class sizes would lead to higher graduation rates and better test scores, only to discover that they did not.[59]

But really, can you blame them? After the announcement of the Newark grant on the Oprah Winfrey show, Winfrey asked Zuckerberg why he was being so generous to a public school district. He replied: "Because every child deserves a good education and right now that's not happening."[60] Of course, self-interest is probably also at work here. The survival of companies like Facebook and Microsoft depends on a well-educated workforce, a thriving economy, and consumers with disposable income.

America's richest citizens and numerous large corporations annually contribute millions of dollars to Teach for America, a well-meaning program that brings talented young people to teach at underperforming schools.[61] Even here, the jury is still out and, 26 years after its founding, many people question a model that seems unsustainable given its high turnover rate.[62] In early 2015, the organization warned that the size of its teaching corps come autumn could be down by as much as a quarter.[63] The number of new applicants had fallen for a second year, and two of its eight national summer training facilities had to be closed.[64]

America is still trying President George W. Bush's No Child Left Behind (NCLB), an expansive national reform effort that many people today view as deeply flawed.[65] NCLB was designed to raise education standards and close achievement gaps, particularly of disadvantaged students, by requiring states to use standardized tests to assess students' reading and math skills, and ultimately get all students performing at grade level. By 2014, every single public school student in America was expected to meet or exceed state standards.[66] That did not happen and now most states are operating under a NCLB waiver, which is essentially a permission slip allowing states to change their accountability formulas.[67] Today, most policy makers agree that the goals were unrealistic.

NCLB is extremely costly. It is the largest federally funded program supporting elementary and secondary education.[68] In fiscal year 2014, more than $14 billion was dedicated to NCLB's biggest program—financial assistance for local educational agencies and schools to boost academic achievement of students from low-income families. (This figure does not include billions more spent annually funding related NCLB programs.)[69] State-level implementation is expensive as well, and has at times stressed budgets to a degree that schools have had to cut programs to educate children—ironically undermining a state's ability to meet NCLB goals.

The latest reform idea is the Common Core State Standards Initiative (the Common Core, as it is known). It is the most recent attempt to boost student achievement nationwide by establishing national academic standards in math and English literacy. Most states quickly adopted the college- and career-ready standards, because doing so made them eligible for federal Race to the Top money,[70] but whether the new standards and accompanying tests will have any significant impact over the long term is anyone's guess. Already there is a backlash, with parents opting their children out of the testing, arguing that the tests are complicated and confusing and that the program is dominating the curriculum at the expense of other subjects.[71] Meanwhile, some experts say there is no proof that setting national standards boosts achievement. They recommend that officials should focus instead on reforms with a better track record of improving student success.[72]

More than twenty years ago, another education reform initiative got underway when some states adopted legislation creating public charter schools. The idea was to cut bureaucracy, increase accountability, and raise the academic standards of public schools. Charter schools operate like public schools, but with a greater degree of autonomy in exchange for a higher level of accountability.

Some of these schools have failed and have been shut down, yet so many more have significantly transformed young lives and strengthened neighborhoods by introducing quality schools in low-income areas, which helps to curb middle-class flight. The statistics (explained in chapter 4) suggest the reform is working too, as they show that charter schools dramatically improve the academic performance of the nation's most disadvantaged children, including low-income black and Hispanic students, as well as English Language Learners[73]—the very students the current system typically fails.[74]

Parents, for their part, have made it clear that they support a reform that gives them an active say in where their children go to school. What these parents of children in low-performing schools want most is not more tinkering, but options other than the one failing school in their neighborhood. In October 2014, tens of thousands of parents and their children publicly rallied in New York City to get the attention of the city's mayor, Bill de Blasio, an opponent of school choice who had denied

Photo 1.1 Families at the New York City rally supporting charter schools in October 2014. Source: Photo by William Farrington / Polaris. Reproduced with permission.

public space to charter schools. At the time, there were some 143,000 of New York City's 1.1 million public school students trapped in "failing" schools, the protesting parents said.[75, 76] "That's not a statistic, that's a crisis," said New York Assemblyman Robert Rodriguez.[77]

Charter schools' biggest critics tend to portray the entire school choice movement as one fueled by greed and driven by wealthy individuals out to profit from kids. While there probably are some people like that, for each one of them there are tens of thousands more like the parents in New York who simply want better schools for their children. "Here's what scares me," said Ebony Burrowes, a parent at the school choice rally in New York. "We know the reality for black men. If my son continues in a school that closes doors for him, I face the reality of him becoming a statistic. I face visiting my son in prison. I face burying my son."[78]

Kenneth Campbell, a founding board member of the Black Alliance for Educational Options, which helps low-income and working-class black families choose higher quality education options for their children, says that the sad reality is that we live in a country where children of color and of low-income parents fare far worse than their peers academically.

The fact is that people with money have options in terms of where and how their kids are educated. We should not live in an America where they are the only people who have that option. We can and should extend some of that power to low-income and minority families.

The larger point I am making is that education reforms to date have not resulted in improved standards across the board. Meanwhile, a lack of access to higher quality educational options is condemning far too many American youth to lives of economic and social oblivion.

More than thirty years ago, the authors of *A Nation at Risk* wrote that the U.S. had an education crisis and noted that roughly 13 percent of American 17-year-olds could be considered functionally illiterate, meaning they would find it challenging to fill out a driver's license application.[79] Today, that number for high school seniors is more like 25 percent, and for black and Hispanic students, it is 44 percent and 36 percent, respectively[80]—all while U.S. spending on public education has skyrocketed.

Given the gravity of the situation, why not employ the one option that has made America great? The U.S. leapt ahead of other countries because it opposed state monopolies in crucial sectors such as telecommunications, transportation, and power generation and instead used the free market to spur competition, creativity, and excellence. Why, then, when it comes to something as important as education, are those lessons lost? It is time to reconsider the nation's education strategy. It is time to seriously engage for-profit help.

CHAPTER 2

Limiting options in a time of crisis

AS THE U.S. POPULATION EXPANDS, enrollment is increasing at public elementary and secondary schools, putting more strain on already struggling schools. Enrollment at public elementary and secondary schools increased 7 percent between 1997 and 2011 and is expected to rise another 7 percent to nearly 53 million students by 2022.[1] Some states will be harder hit than others. As an example, in Nevada—a state already dealing with a serious student homelessness problem[2, 3]—public school student populations are predicted to balloon by more than 22 percent between 2004 and 2022.[4]

The demographic makeup of these bigger student populations makes things more challenging as well. Public classrooms increasingly include a larger percentage of students from low-income families,[5] of Hispanic origin, and who are not native English speakers[6]—all representing historically underachieving groups. This trend is expected to continue, with the percentage of Hispanic students, for example, estimated to rise 33 percent between 2011 and 2022.[7]

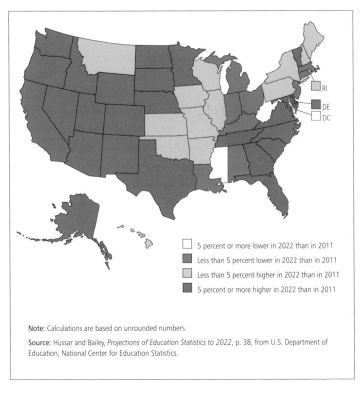

Figure 2.1 Projected percentage change in enrollment in public elementary and secondary schools, by state: fall 2011 through fall 2022[8]

Poverty has also become a big challenge for U.S. public schools. Between 2000 and 2012 there was a 40 percent jump in the poverty rate of school-age children, according to the National Center for Education Statistics.[9] Students from low-income families now represent the majority of public school students, according to a 2015 study from the Southern Education Foundation.[10] Meanwhile, the number of homeless students across America hit a record high of 1.26 million in 2013, according to U.S. Department of Education data released in late 2014.[11] These trends present a huge challenge for educators as the achievement gap between high-income and low-income students has widened significantly over the past three decades.[12]

If achievement gaps between these various groups are not seriously addressed, there will be grave implications for the U.S. economy. Low-income and minority students are less likely to go to college than their peers and have traditionally been underrepresented in critical fields such as science, medicine, and engineering.[13] It is obvious that a growing percentage of historically underachieving students does not bode well for America's future.

So, what are lawmakers doing to prepare for this more challenging future? Given the gravity of the situation you would think they would push to improve education standards by using every means possible, including embracing for-profit companies that can build great schools. Instead, far too many of them are playing politics.

In Michigan—a state with 232 charter schools serving more than 100,000 students[14]—some Democratic lawmakers in 2014 called for a moratorium on new charter schools. They said they had questions about these schools' transparency and accountability. Yet, with a Republican-controlled legislature, the proposal had no hope of passing, and even some Democrats said that a moratorium would eliminate quality alternatives for kids in districts with bad public schools.[15] So why did they bother?

"This proposal was a political stunt carried out in a tight election year to get a Democrat candidate elected as governor," explains Todd Ziebarth, senior vice president for state advocacy and support for the National Alliance for Public Charter Schools. (Ultimately, the proposal gained so little traction that it never came to a vote, he adds.)

The Michigan lawmakers took particular aim at charter schools managed by for-profit companies. Attacking for-profit education providers is a popular strategy used by some legislators. Sometimes, lawmakers sacrifice for-profits to appease opponents in order to pass controversial school reforms. It is a relatively painless sacrifice as for-profits manage fewer than 13 percent of all charter schools nationwide,[16] so dispensing with them does not end charter schools.

For-profits also represent less of a political threat to lawmakers. Far from being big, greedy corporate types, as portrayed by critics, most for-profit education providers are small companies, according to the National Education Policy Center,[17] and so wield far less political might than school unions, and also less than nonprofit education providers, which can be backed by extremely influential philanthropists. No politician wants to alienate a Gates or a Walton. As of May 2015, seven states restricted or banned for-profit companies from managing public schools, and many other state lawmakers have proposed doing the same.[18]

Some legislators and public school officials vilify for-profit charter school operators even in states and districts where there is no question that these schools are effectively educating children. In Camden, New Jersey, where one in four students attends a charter school, the superintendent of schools for the city in 2014 came out against for-profits, while at the same time saying he would work with the only for-profit operated school in his district because it was doing a good job.[19] "They're serving kids, and those kids deserve a good education," said

Superintendent Paymon Rouhanifard, according to the *South Jersey Times*. "But I don't think there is as much of a place for an organization that is there explicitly to make a profit. I think that's a little bit trickier."[20]

For-profits make easy targets in part because the arguments against them sound so virtuous. Critics argue that public education is a public responsibility and that it must be protected from market forces. Some go a step further saying that the nation's very freedom depends on it. But ask any parent whose child is stuck in a failing inner-city school just how free he or she feels.

Some opponents use the emotionally charged claim that for-profits will cut corners to profit from children. This sounds plausible, yet if you press people to further explain their concerns, they fall short. Often they will say things like: "These companies take public tax dollars but aren't transparent or accountable to the public about how the money is spent." The problem is that this assertion is not true. On the contrary, the for-profit companies that manage charter schools are transparent by law, and in many ways are far more accountable to the public than traditional public schools.

Here are some of the rules:

■ All charter schools must meet state and federal academic achievement standards, just like traditional public schools.[21]

■ Companies that run charter schools are treated just like any other government contractor, so regulatory oversight applies.

■ Charter schools are funded with public dollars and so

35

are subject to regular audits and ongoing reviews from authorizing entities to show how taxpayer dollars are spent.[22]

- Charter schools have contracts with charter authorizing bodies that establish rigorous academic, financial, and managerial standards, which the schools must meet to keep operating.[23]

- With for-profits, there is the additional scrutiny of their finances and management practices by their own shareholders.

- If charter schools fail to meet the criteria set forth in foundational charter agreements, they can be shut down,[24] unlike many traditional public schools, which can undergo ineffective turnaround procedures for years while failing generations of students.

The notion that for-profits can operate in any manner they choose using taxpayer money is incorrect, as is the claim that for-profits are something new in education. For-profits have long played an integral role in public education. For-profits supply computers, books, school lunches, landscaping and janitorial services, and numerous other essential goods and services. And yet there are few people accusing companies like Google or Microsoft or Pearson (a publicly listed British company and leading supplier of educational materials in the U.S.) of cutting corners to make profits from children.

For-profits also play a crucial role in early childhood public education. Since 1995, states have funded pre-school education programs.[25] Most states have public pre-kindergarten programs that allow participation by for-profit childcare providers, using taxpayer money.[26] Essentially, this means that while it is fine for for-profit companies to educate and care for children during their most formative years, it is a problem when they go to elementary school and high school. My point is that the arguments against for-profit management of public schools are disingenuous.

For-profits are stigmatized even in states where they play key roles in public education. In Nashville, Tennessee, for example, the school district contracted with a for-profit company to handle special education needs in its public schools, as many districts around the country have done in order to reduce special education spending.[27] Yet a Tennessee state statute specifically prohibits charter governing boards from contracting with for-profits to manage or operate charter schools. Kara Kerwin, president of the advocacy group the Center for Education Reform, says this is hypocritical: "They had a for-profit entity running the whole division of a traditional public school system, yet a charter school board couldn't contract with a for-profit provider to help them manage and run their school," she says.

As the charter movement has progressed, arguments against for-profit management companies have grown more outlandish. The most vocal opponents say that for-profits are out to undermine teachers and destroy public schools. Then there are those who warn of a threat to democracy.

Let me first address the claim that charter schools undermine teachers. The usual flawed assertion is that charter schools employ unqualified teachers and pay them less, thus lowering the quality of teaching everywhere. Yet, a provision of the No Child Left Behind Act requires all teachers at public schools, including charter schools, to be "highly qualified,"[28] making this point moot. While it is true that most charter schools are free to pay a market rate, it is not true that this flexibility should undermine anyone. On the contrary, the tenure system and other job protections offered in most states[29] to public school teachers can seriously undermine the needs of students by making it difficult to remove teachers who cannot teach and making it hard to reward and promote those teachers who can.

More than three decades ago, the authors of *A Nation at Risk* said that teacher protections had to be addressed in order to fix failing schools.[30] The authors wrote: "Salary, promotion, tenure, and retention decisions should be tied to an effective evaluation system that includes peer review so that superior teachers can be rewarded, average ones encouraged, and poor ones either improved or terminated."[31] While some school districts have moved toward performance pay (embracing an idea that rewards teachers) special interest groups like teachers unions have fiercely resisted changes that threaten their personal interests, including lengthening the school year or loosening job protections such as tenure rules.[32]

There was one bright spot in 2014 when a Los Angeles trial court judge ruled in *Vergara v. California* that laws governing teacher tenure and other job protections violated the state's constitution—not to mention the students' fundamental right to equality of education.[33] The lawsuit, filed on behalf of nine public school students in 2012, argued that the tenure system was deeply flawed in California and meant that even grossly incompetent teachers were hard to dismiss.[34] According to testimony, only 91 teachers in California had been fired over the past ten years, and only 19 for unsatisfactory performance, while another witness during the trial said that between 2,750 and 8,250 California teachers were ranked as grossly ineffective.[35] A big part of the problem is that school leaders must decide whether to grant tenure to teachers by the spring of these new teachers' second year—often before it is clear whether they can even teach.[36] The process required to fire tenured teachers—even grossly incompetent ones—is extremely challenging, time-consuming, and costly.[37] The California lawsuit drew national attention when the judge ruled in favor of the plaintiffs, agreeing that teacher protections, including tenure, violated the civil rights of students in the state because the worst teachers taught in the highest poverty schools, resulting in unequal conditions.[38] While the verdict could be overturned on appeal, the tide may be turning as similar lawsuits have followed in favor of putting students' needs over teacher security. Finally.

Next, let me respond to the idea that charter schools, and for-profits in particular, destroy public education. Critics claim that charter schools are detrimental to public education because they siphon off much-needed funds from school districts. They also claim that unscrupulous business types will take the public's money to build unregulated and unaccountable schools.

Let me address the money issue first. This money belongs to the students, not the districts, and students who attend charter schools are public school students. A reasonable person might ask why taxpayers should give money to school districts that fail to adequately educate students. As for destroying public education, I want to be clear about this: The people at the heart of the charter school movement have never suggested eliminating, much less destroying, public schools, or deregulating the public education system or making schools unaccountable.

Rather, the goal is a simple one: To give parents viable alternatives to failing schools.

Frankly, I have no idea what people mean when they say that charter schools undermine democracy. Giving parents a choice of education providers can hardly be said to threaten a democratic state designed to give people equal rights and privileges, along with the right to decide for themselves on matters as important as their children's education.

It is public school districts that operate less freely and are in essence monopolies run by bureaucrats who are not answerable to consumers (parents and students). It should surprise no one that quality is a problem. Monopolies rarely deliver high quality products and services. Yet, many people continue to place excessive faith in districts that consistently fail to adequately educate children. On the other hand, if a for-profit education management company provides a bad service, the students stop coming, the school loses money, and eventually it shuts down even if the charter has not been revoked. Yes, some students are temporarily displaced, and that is not a good thing, but I would argue that it is better than being stuck in a perennially underperforming school.

The entire argument over whether an operating entity is for-profit or not is irrelevant, says Anne Kandilis, a member of the governing board at our school in Springfield, Massachusetts, and a former partner at a "Big Four" accounting firm.

My feeling is that as long as the price is fair, you're producing a product that can be measured and it's transparent, I don't care if it's for-profit or nonprofit. May the best business entity win. I think you have to understand who's going to produce the product you want—graduating kids who are proficient and who have a choice to go to college—and then you should be

*measured on those results. It's really about results. It's naïve
to think that for-profit and nonprofit makes a difference.*

Instead of haggling over the tax status of education
providers, politicians should be giving preference to those
providers who deliver the best value for money, just as with
any other government contractor.

As it stands, charter schools often do more, and do more
with less. University of Arkansas researchers found that
in 2011, school districts received $3,509 more on average
per pupil than charter schools.[39] With less public funding,
charter schools usually supply their own teaching materials,
provide teacher training, must find their own outside contractors, and are far more demanding about costs. No charter
school operator—and certainly no for-profit one—would pay
hundreds of dollars over retail per iPad, as happened in the
Los Angeles public schools.[40] Nor are they likely to build a
so-called Taj Mahal school building, like the more than half a
billion dollar Robert F. Kennedy Community Schools complex
in Los Angeles, unveiled at a time when the district was
running a $640 million deficit that required laying off a few
thousand teachers.[41] Shareholders in a for-profit education
company would never permit such profligate spending.

For-profit-managed charter schools offer taxpayers
even more value for their money because they use private
dollars for a public good, such as building infrastructure
in run-down neighborhoods. Nonprofit-managed charter
schools use private capital too, but for-profits (not dependent
on the goodwill of donors) are typically better at marshaling
resources and have greater access to capital. A successful for-
profit model also has the advantage of being able to expand

and become self-sustaining with its own capital. Dan Quisen-berry, president of the Michigan Association of Public School Academies (MAPSA), says that often this financial benefit is overlooked. "People demonize the fact that there are these for-profit people involved in providing a public service," he says. "We shouldn't be discouraging this. We ought to be encour-aging this. It's an enormous savings to taxpayers."

People also tend to overlook the fact that good charter schools curb urban flight of middle-class families in inner-city neighborhoods and eventually help revitalize these cities. Just ask Raipher Pellegrino. He is a lawyer who in the mid-1990s served on the city council in Springfield, Massachusetts. It was his swing vote that approved a lease on a building that eventu-ally helped SABIS to get its first charter in the state. Pellegrino says it was a difficult decision to make as his sister and aunts were teachers in the public school system and were all union members. He later joined the school's board and his four children graduated from the school. Looking back, Pellegrino says it was the best vote he ever made on the city council because, by giving the district a good school, many middle-income taxpayers did not flee to the suburbs. "By voting 'yes,' I helped stabilize the upper middle class from moving out of Springfield," he says.

Please don't misunderstand me. I am not saying that when it comes to educating children the primary focus ought to be about short-term financial savings or even inner-city regen-eration. I am saying that the preference should be toward those providers who give the best value for money.

For-profits offer another distinct advantage: Scalability. Nonprofit education providers must rely on the goodwill of philanthropists, while successful for-profits attract money from investors looking for returns, making it easier to expand their models. Over seven years, Tom Pritchard, founding chairman of the board of KIPP Metro Atlanta, a nonprofit charter school network of eight schools in Georgia, helped the chain raise more than $30 million but says it was extraordinarily challenging. "It's difficult to scale anything that doesn't have a for-profit motive," he explains. "I realize people will be able to quote examples to the contrary, but I would suggest that those are outlier examples."

Having a large pool of ready cash is crucial, particularly when it comes to infrastructure. A company will be awarded a charter, but decisions by officials regarding school buildings often get delayed, and companies have no control over what kind of shape the buildings are in or how much money is required to repair them. In the meantime, education companies (or charter school boards, which are sometimes responsible for buildings) must line up alternative facilities in case the district building fails to come through. Pritchard recalls an instance in which the KIPP nonprofit network was awarded a building just eight weeks ahead of the school's opening date. It had not been used in years and was in terrible shape, so they had to scramble to raise money at the last minute to fix it up before the start of the school year. For-profits often have the advantage of being able to line up cash ahead of time and are less exposed to this type of risk.

Pritchard, who has also invested in for-profit education companies, says that philanthropists prefer not to provide unlimited funding for operations. They would rather fund more tangible things like computers or buildings. Nor are their funds unlimited; you can approach them only so many times. For-profits have a big advantage, adds Pritchard.

They would have an investor base who has signed off on a plan. They already have the money that they think they are going to need. We have to go out and raise the money quickly under very adverse circumstances with very little time to do it, from a funding community that often is reluctant to provide the amount and type of money we are seeking.

Former tennis star Andre Agassi created a nonprofit charter school in Las Vegas, but soon realized his philanthropic approach would have limited impact because of the constant challenges to raise money. He teamed up with social impact investor Bobby Turner to set up the Turner–Agassi Charter School Facilities Fund, which finances the building of charter school facilities across the country. "I don't believe, personally, that philanthropy is scalable," Agassi has said.[42]

During a tour in 2014 of a new facility in Nashville, Tennessee, Turner said that "neither philanthropy nor the government are particularly good at actually curing problems," adding that they can be unreliable, inefficient, ineffective, and also lacking in accountability.

From my background as a capitalist—I know that may be offensive—I recognize that the only way to truly cure a problem in society is to create a sustainable solution, harnessing market forces to make money. The reality is, there's no secret: Making money and making societal change need not be [mutually] exclusive.[43]

The notion that public interest is served best by individuals pursuing self-interest has long been conventional wisdom in America. In fact, the nation's refusal to impose state monopolies in public sectors such as telecommunications, transportation, and power utilities, and embrace a free market instead, is a key reason for its economic success. Indeed, globally, it is not communism that reigns, but a free market system that combines a profit motive and competition. This free market thinking, which influenced early American leaders, can be found in Adam Smith's *Wealth of Nations*, first published in 1776:[44]

> *It is not from the benevolence of the butcher, the brewer, or the baker that we expect our dinner, but from their regard to their own interest. We address ourselves, not to their humanity but to their self-love, and never talk to them of our own necessities but of their advantages.*

In other words, people should care less about the baker's motivation to bake bread, or whether there is any money in it, and more about whether the baker's bread is any good. The idea should be to have as many bakers as possible to encourage competition and ultimately improve quality.

Public education is the last holdout in a long American story involving the mobilization of private sector resources to overcome serious social challenges. Frankly, it is strange in a country that has long relied on for-profit enterprises to build essential services, including energy, transportation, telecommunications, and health, that opponents of private sector involvement in public schools have gained so much traction.

In the end, what should matter most is that these schools work, are held to task, and ultimately deliver results—a quality education to a growing student body with a greater complexity of needs. Any reasonable person can see that the tax status of the provider should be irrelevant if a school can show results.

CHAPTER 3

Hurdles and roadblocks

IN THE EARLY 1990s, U.S. public education was in crisis. Too many schools were failing to adequately educate students without being held accountable. In response, lawmakers in various states passed legislation to permit private sector companies to run public schools. Education management had traditionally been off limits to the private sector, but state leaders recognized that public schools needed outside help to make them more competitive and to raise standards. To ensure organizations would be held accountable and produce results, they made sure that the awarded charters could be revoked.

The organizations (some for-profit, some not) were granted unprecedented freedom and autonomy to run public schools in order to shake up the system and turn things around. In return for meeting academic, financial, and managerial goals laid out in charters (as well as meeting state and federal education standards), these education providers could use their own state-aligned curriculum, lengthen the school day and school year, hire whomever they pleased (regardless of whether they had a teaching certificate), and generally be free of the kinds of school rules that were not necessarily working.

Presidential proclamation

These institutions [charter schools] give educators the freedom to cultivate new teaching models and develop creative methods to meet students' needs. This unique flexibility is matched by strong accountability and high standards, so underperforming charter schools can be closed, while those that consistently help students succeed can serve as models of reform for other public schools.

In an economy where knowledge is our most valuable asset, a good education is no longer just a pathway to opportunity—it is an imperative. Our children only get one chance at an education, and charter schools demonstrate what is possible when States, communities, teachers, parents, and students work together.

President Barack Obama, *A Proclamation by the President of the United States of America*, May 7, 2012[1]

While no reform is perfect, it is safe to say that the model has largely been successful and is getting more so over time. Demand for charter schools outstrips supply across the country, with most schools reporting waiting lists with hundreds of names,[2] and the largest charter school study out of Stanford University demonstrates obvious improvement by charter school students over time.[3] What is extraordinary, though, is how much progress charter schools have made despite opponents doing everything in their power to destroy them.

Since the earliest days of the reform, charter school opponents (people threatened most by the success of charter schools, including members of teachers unions, legislators beholden to teachers unions, most school district officials, and others with entrenched interests in preserving the status quo) have aggressively pushed a political agenda that discourages healthy competition in the public education sector and that forces charter schools to compete on a hugely uneven playing field. As of May 2015, lawmakers in seven states had yet to pass laws permitting charter schools to exist,[4] while some states with charter school laws still allow only nonprofit education providers to run these schools. Among the dozens of states (including Washington, D.C.) that welcome a variety of education providers including for-profits,[5] too few feature the kinds of rules and regulations to help the reform flourish, such as more freedom to expand and innovate, and equitable funding and facilities support.

While there has been progress in some states, most still impose a crippling array of operating restrictions, such as limits on growth, lower funding for students—30 percent less in some states[6]—limited, if any, funding for facilities, random authorizing procedures, and a contract renewal process that is bureaucratic and subjective and too often includes a contract period that is too short to adequately measure progress.

Bad policies scare off good companies that could dramatically improve public education. In our early days in Massachusetts in the 1990s, there were nearly half a dozen other for-profit education providers. Today SABIS is the only one left, and if you ask the head of the Massachusetts Charter Public School Association in Massachusetts, Marc Kenen, he will say it is mainly because most companies simply cannot make a go of it given the many restrictions. Ultimately, these bad policies rob parents of higher quality educational options for their children and undermine a valuable system of reform that legislators wrote into law more than two decades ago.

Some rules result from bad policy decisions by well-meaning people, but more often than not, these legislative hurdles and roadblocks are created and championed by adversaries intent on undermining the charter school movement and killing off all for-profit involvement.

First, I would like to talk about growth restrictions, which opponents use to limit charter school development. Nation-wide, more than 600,000 students are on charter school waiting lists,[7] representing nearly a quarter of the number of students already at these schools, and yet, as of May 2015, 22 states (including the District of Columbia) limited the number of charter schools and the percentage of students who can attend them.[8]

Why most public school officials push for these restric-tions is not hard to figure out. School districts only have so many students and funding follows each one of them. More students choosing charter schools means less money for public school districts. Add to that the fact that bright and motivated students, and good teachers too, are among those leaving traditional public schools for charter schools.

This is probably why caps on growth exist even in states with particularly high demand for more charter schools. Massachusetts, for example, restricts the number of charter schools and students attending them, even though, in 2014, nearly 45,000 students in the state were on waiting lists to attend them. If the cap were eliminated, charter school enroll-ment would more than double in the state.[9] (There is hope that the Massachusetts cap will be overturned. In March 2015, lawyers filed a constitutional challenge against the cap, arguing that students were being denied the right to a quality education.)[10]

State law in Illinois, which had almost 30,000 more applications by students for charter schools in 2013 than available charter school places,[11] limits the number of charter schools to 120. Andrew Broy, president of the Illinois Network of Charter Schools, says that such restrictions may have made sense twenty years ago when charter schools were new and unproven, "but the argument gets more time worn over the years."

Here is a look at charter school supply versus demand in Illinois.[12]

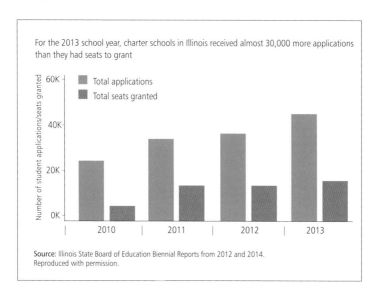

For the 2013 school year, charter schools in Illinois received almost 30,000 more applications than they had seats to grant

Source: Illinois State Board of Education Biennial Reports from 2012 and 2014. Reproduced with permission.

Figure 3.1 Charter school supply versus demand in Illinois, 2013

Caps are debated in legislatures every year in some states, and to avoid them, charter school advocates are often forced to make sacrifices. Opponents use the issue as leverage to eliminate charter school advantages such as autonomy and freedom—the very things granted to charter schools to make them more competitive. A compromise in 2009 made it easier for charter school teachers to unionize in Illinois, says Broy, while in 2006, advocates in the state acquiesced to a new rule requiring teacher certification for 75 percent of charter school academic staff.[13] As an aside, opponents often demand certification for charter school teachers, even though there is a serious shortage of teachers nationwide, particularly in critical areas such as science, technology, engineering, and mathematics.[14]

Indeed, across the nation, a movement is well underway to make charter schools just like traditional public schools, seemingly in an effort to neutralize them. Charter schools have become a fact of life, with more than 6,700 nationwide educating about 2.9 million students, as of February 2015.[15] The theory of some opponents must be: If you cannot beat them, make them just like you—less competitive.

Sometimes it is well-meaning advocates of the movement that undercut charter schools by interfering. In Arizona, for example, a charter school association asked the state to require charter school teachers to participate in the association's professional development program for their schools to qualify for particular grants, even though charter schools typically have their own training methods and the recommended "cookie-cutter" approach was not appropriate, says Jeanne Allen, founder of the Center for Education Reform. Allen says that requirements such as these are made in dozens of communities and states across the country, though typically it is school district officials who chip away at charter school freedoms, or "in other words, are moving schools more towards the exact system that they tried to get away from."

Often the issue is about control. Forcing all schools to follow the same rules, such as those governing teacher training, gives district officials greater authority over charter schools. But at other times it is about undermining the pledges and goals in education management companies' charters. In Illinois, for example, school choice opponents won a battle to force charter schools to use the state's English Language Learner curriculum, according to Broy of the Illinois Network of Charter Schools. These changes, which came into effect in 2014, eliminated the ability of charter schools to design their own programs, which in many cases were better tailored to students' needs. They also cut the hours of instruction available to English Language Learner students, thereby undercutting the goals in the schools' charter applications. "What you're seeing is an anti-charter coalition coming together to stop charters in their tracks, and these are the techniques they're using to do it," says Broy.

Even the freedom to discipline students in ways operators think best is under attack. In 2014, a local school board in Chicago tried to pass a rule to force charter schools to use the same disciplinary system used by traditional public schools. It seems a strange stand to take in Chicago, home of some of America's most dangerous schools. "The position of the charter community is this: The system you're using is not producing orderly schools in your district and so why impose a broken system on us?" says Broy. The measure did not pass, but in 2015 it was back on the table again.

One of the funniest attempts—if it weren't so sad—to show that charter schools could be run just like traditional public schools involved the United Federation of Teachers (UFT) union. In 2005, the union created its own charter school in

Brooklyn to prove that reform could flourish under union terms, including under the city's union contract. It did not. Instead, the UFT charter school was plagued for a decade by fiscal problems and high principal turnover, and in 2014 was one of a handful of schools citywide to miss meeting four out of five set goals, with grades kindergarten through eighth failing in areas including those related to student achievement and closing the achievement gap, reported *The Wall Street Journal*.[16]

James Merriman, chief executive officer (CEO) of the New York City Charter School Center, which advocates for high quality charters, called the school's results "just sad," adding in an interview with *The Wall Street Journal*: "Given the school was supposed to be a proof point for union expertise, for the UFT to let it fail so badly strikes me as educational and political malpractice."[17] As a charter school advocate, Merriman is not a disinterested party, but the school's results speak for themselves. In late February 2015, the union announced it would close the elementary and middle schools, but would ask the state to renew its charter for grades 9 through 12.[18]

Of all of the hurdles thrown up by opponents, the most effective at keeping for-profit talent from entering public education are those related to the most fundamental charter school opening and operating procedures. These include roadblocks connected to the funding of students and facilities, authorization of new charters, and contract renewals.

Let me start by addressing the chronic inequalities related to student funding. I mentioned earlier that a study from the University of Arkansas found that in 2011 school districts received on average $3,509 more per pupil than charter schools.[19] What I did not say was that this gap has grown significantly in recent years. University of Arkansas researchers wrote that between 2003 and 2011 the gap grew by 54.5 percent (adjusted for inflation), while charter school enrollment increased in every state and in Washington, D.C.,[20] despite efforts by opponents to tighten enrollment caps.

This equity gap is higher in urban areas, where, on average, traditional public schools received $4,352 more per pupil than charter schools.[21] The need to supply equal funding for students, particularly students with greater needs, could not be more obvious. These charter school students are public school students, yet those who choose one particular government-sanctioned option—charter schools—are being discriminated against.

In some states, parents and charter school advocates are suing over this unequal funding.[22] Lawyers on behalf of five families from Buffalo and Rochester, New York, filed a lawsuit in September 2014 claiming that chronic funding gaps violate the state's constitution and disproportionately hurt minority students.[23] The suit says that charter school students during the 2010–11 school year in the Buffalo school district received around $9,800 less per student than their peers at traditional public schools, while charter school students in Rochester received about $6,600 less.[24]

Across the state of New York, evidence suggests that traditional public school students receive roughly 30 percent more funding than charter school students.[25] This hardly seems fair, given that nearly 80 percent of New York's charter school students are from low-income homes, while 93 percent are students of color, according to the lawsuit.[26]

A similar lawsuit was filed in Washington, D.C. in July 2014 against the school district and the mayor, claiming that the city seriously underfunded charter school students, with a

Photo 3.1 Charter school students, teachers, parents, and supporters in Hawaii rally legislators to support more funding for their schools.

Source: Photo by Melvin Ah Ching. Reproduced with permission.

shortfall since 2008 totaling more than $770 million.[27] This funding gap breaks the law, claim representatives of charter schools, and hurts charter school students, who represent about 44 percent of all public school students in the district.[28]

The suit also argues that money is allocated unfairly.[29] Funds for charter schools are based on confirmed enrollments, while funds for traditional public schools are based on estimates of enrollment for the coming year.[30] These estimates, according to the lawsuit, are inflated, as enrollment at traditional public schools in Washington, D.C. has been steadily declining and the numbers do not reflect that.[31] Of course, court battles like these could drag on for years and ultimately fail to change anything.

In the meantime, the charter movement continues to

expand, despite this financial disparity. Between the 2008–9 and 2013–14 school years, student enrollment at charter schools nationwide grew by 70 percent.[32] In the 2014–15 school year alone, almost 500 new charter schools opened,[33] while the number of new students at charter schools rose 14 percent from the previous school year to reach a total of about 2.9 million students.[34] Yet growth could be even faster.

One of the biggest obstacles to growth is a lack of funding for facilities. Most charter schools do not receive funding to cover the costs of securing and maintaining facilities, while traditional public schools get both types of funding. Only four jurisdictions (California, Colorado, Washington, D.C., and Utah) offer equitable access to capital funding and facilities,[35] while only 16 states provide per pupil funding specifically earmarked for facilities, with only three jurisdictions (Arizona, Minnesota, and Washington, D.C.) providing more than $1,000 on a per pupil basis.[36]

But even in those states that provide some facilities funding, it is not nearly enough to cover the full costs of renting, purchasing, or maintaining school facilities. Charter schools instead generally rely on donor grants to build and maintain facilities or seek traditional loans or bond financing.

Sometimes education companies provide a facility as part of their service. SABIS does not ordinarily do this, but in 1999, when our students needed a new building in Springfield, Massachusetts, we took a huge risk by putting up SABIS's own assets as collateral to finance one. It worked out, thanks to the hard work and effort of a lot of people, and the governing board of the SABIS International Charter School (SICS) now owns the building. However, we would much prefer to focus on students than on real estate transactions.

Compounding the problem is a lack of access nationwide to public bond financing, the low-cost option used by state and municipal governments to construct public facilities. Without government help, charter schools pay significantly higher rates of interest on the open market, using public dollars. Banks tend to gouge charter school lenders, and it is hard to blame them, given the risks involved with a short, five-year contract and no guarantee of renewal.

Some lawmakers have recognized these problems, and there has been progress such as states making bond financing more affordable for charter schools by letting them directly or indirectly issue tax-exempt bonds, as local school districts can do. It is worth noting, though, that this option is usually only available to schools with a track record, and not to start-up charter schools.

Some states have gone a step further. Utah lawmakers, for example, authorized a general obligation pledge tied to the taxing authority, which gave schools borrowing with this pledge a double-A rating and dramatically lowered their borrowing costs.[37]

As welcome as moves like these are, many challenges related to facilities funding remain. Too few lawmakers have focused on this facilities issue and removed obstacles. Some state education officials are not particularly cooperative either when it comes to helping schools identify vacant properties. Buying buildings is problematic, as again, a five-year charter contract is not a long enough period over which to finance a facility, much less buy land and build a facility. If you are a new school, forget about traditional bank financing, as banks view new charter schools as too risky. Making matters worse is the fact that school boards of directors, who are often the lessee or owner and who have no prior track record that can be evaluated by underwriters, add to the expense of the project because banks tend to charge them higher interest rates to offset their risk.

Given all of these issues, most charter schools rent properties and typically pay commercial rates on leases to operate out of less than ideal facilities, converting buildings like old churches, offices, and strip malls into schools. There are only so many suitable buildings available in some urban areas.

Still others have to accept less than desirable lease contracts, partly because charter school contracts are so short that they cannot lock in longer-term leases. The problem is exacerbated by the fact that sometimes charters are awarded just months, if not weeks, before a school is expected to open.

Sometimes charter schools (boards or the education providers, as the case may be) take and refurbish buildings they know they will soon outgrow. In other cases, schools settle for locations without good transportation links, making it difficult to attract students and teachers. A lack of transportation, in fact, is a major impediment to enrolling students. For our charter school in Saginaw, Michigan, for example, there is no busing at all, while in Cincinnati, Ohio, buses to our school run at inconvenient times, making it doubly challenging in a community where so few parents own cars.

Meanwhile, traditional public schools are, relatively speaking, flush with cash—or at least have access to cash—as they can typically borrow huge sums of money at favorable terms. The problem is that the money is not necessarily going to the right places, such as to instruct students. In some cases, hundreds of millions of dollars have been spent constructing luxury facilities.

Photo 3.2 Ramón C. Cortines School of Visual and Performing Arts, a public high school in Los Angeles, California, a district with chronic budget shortfalls. Reported cost to build the school: $232 million.[38]

Source: Photo by Nils Koenning. Reproduced with permission.

Glenn Hileman, CEO of Highmark School Development, which helps companies finance and build charter schools around the country, says:

You go see some of these district schools that are being built, and they'll spend $200, $300 or $400 a square foot, where a charter school has to nickel and dime it to a fraction of that, like a third or half of the budget for a facility that serves the same number of students.

So in many regards I would tell you that charter schools are the taxpayers' best friend because the model of charter schools requires a charter school to be more efficient in the deployment of taxpayer dollars on facilities. So when I look around the country and I see these district Taj Mahals, I think it's appalling because they really don't need that unbelievable state-of-the-art atrium or the gymnasium with all the bells and whistles. They can function, and it's been proven that many schools do function, with facilities that are far more efficient.

Next, I would like to talk about the charter school authorization process and two key problems that allow opponents to block charter school growth. Clearly, as with the award of any public contract, the authorization process should be transparent and safeguarded from political influence. Sadly, this is often not the case. Most states lack fully transparent charter application, review, and decision-making processes, making it difficult to see whether charters are awarded on merit.[39] In Kansas, for example, authorizers are not required to conduct in-person interviews, approve or deny applications in a public meeting, or even state their reasons for denial in writing.[40]

Indeed, only one state—Louisiana—boasts a system that meets standards recommended by the National Alliance for Public Charter Schools, a national research and advocacy group. Louisiana requires the public posting of all application forms, timelines, and processes for review, and requires the use of an independent evaluation of the proposal by a third party.[41] Louisiana law also requires that decisions on charter applications be made by formal vote at official meetings of the public entities responsible and requires written explanation of reasons for denial.[42]

The second fundamental flaw with the authorization process relates to who decides which charters are granted. Some states give local school districts (and no other authorizing bodies) the right to approve new charters. This is like asking the owner of a McDonald's if he wants a Burger King next door. School districts are generally hostile to charter schools (i.e., competitors) and so have little incentive to approve them. I am not saying here that local school districts should lose all control over their own districts, but I am saying that they should not be in the sole position to award contracts to potential competitors.

Efforts to create additional entities responsible for authorizing charters are fiercely battled by charter school opponents. A good example is the case I mentioned in the Introduction to this book, concerning a school SABIS ran in Georgia for nearly nine months in 2010 before it was closed over exactly this issue. The Georgia legislature had passed a bill to establish a state commission to authorize new charters, with our school being granted one of them. School district leaders, however, felt they should have sole authorizing power and so appealed to the state's Supreme Court, arguing that the state authorizing entity was unconstitutional. The court sided with district leaders in a 4 to 3 vote. As a result, our charter and several others in the state were deemed to have been illegally granted and were revoked, leaving thousands of students without schools. Charter school supporters responded by proposing an amendment to the constitution, which led to a statewide vote. This popular vote overwhelmingly (59 percent) supported the existence of a state authorizing entity, underscoring the reality that charter schools are generally embraced by the public despite what adversaries may say. Unfortunately, the popular vote came two years after the first court ruling and our school never reopened.

This story illustrates what charter school operators routinely face from opponents. But more than that, it shows that the biggest losers are students. Yes, SABIS lost a significant amount of time and money, but the students and their parents were left scrambling at the final hour to find alternative schools. It was not just the 520 students at our school, or the 90 new students enrolled for the following year, but more than 15,000 kids attending 15 other schools across the state where charters were also revoked over this issue.[43] It is not as if there are a lot of other school options out there either.

Parents at the time (it was summer) demanded that district officials offer a solution, saying that come the new school year, their kids would be waiting outside the schools' front doors. In the end, most of the schools received local or state approval to open, though a few had to close for good, leaving the children and their parents to sort out last-minute alternatives.

If companies manage to clear various funding hurdles and squeeze through a too often biased authorization process, they still have to contend with frequent contract renewals that often feature unclear procedures that vary by state. Like many school operators, I fully support the concept of a charter renewal process that is based on achieved results. A good renewal process is essential to ensuring successful schools. It is here that we operators are held accountable for results and have the chance to review our progress and make sure we are keeping our promises.

The trouble is that all too often the renewal process is unnecessarily bureaucratic, with authorizers demanding masses of information—much of which they already have. Then they send inspectors (who can be outside contractors with limited, if any, school operating experience) who often submit subjective opinions even when contradictory, hard evidence has already been submitted.

I also take issue with the frequency of such reviews. A five-year term essentially means an analysis on four years of performance or less, depending on when the renewal applications are due and the availability of performance data. In some cases schools are being evaluated on as little as two years' performance. Even a four-year period is too short to gauge performance, particularly with a new school at which enrollment is still growing and with so many entering students performing academically far below grade level. Financially, a new school would hardly be up to speed either, as four years is not enough time to build the enrollment necessary to create long-term financial stability.

Too often, the decision-making process during renewal is cloudy—nowhere near the clarity of the measures to which operators are held accountable—and again, political. (I'll come back to this in chapter 5.)

Of course, when all else fails to detract talent from the sector, there is always the nuclear option in which opponents call for moratoriums on new charter schools. In recent years, opponents nationwide have called for legislation to prohibit new charter schools from opening. They say that they are concerned about accountability and transparency (things dictated in legislation and answered in charter applications) and need time to review the situation. This has happened in Delaware, Illinois, Indiana, Maine, Michigan, New Hampshire, New Jersey, and New Mexico.

Often, such moves are designed to score political points, as in Michigan, where, as I mentioned before, some lawmakers proposed a moratorium, knowing it would never pass the Republican-controlled state senate. As it turned out, it did not even come to a vote.

The language surrounding moratoriums can be conveniently vague, as was the case in Michigan, where critics pointed out that the proposed bill lacked a deadline for when the moratorium would be lifted and clarity over what charter school operators needed to do to end it.[44]

Opponents calling for moratoriums are basically advocating a wait-and-see approach two decades after the opening of the first charter school. This kind of obstructive behavior is not helpful. In the interest of everyone, the focus at this point should be on identifying the most successful charter school models, regardless of whether they are for-profit models or nonprofit, and trying to replicate them, as well as working to enact legislation that would support the proliferation of the highest quality charter schools. Better legislation would also serve to attract more competitors, thereby forcing ineffective operators out of the market.

It is fair to say here that there have been some bad charter schools. There is no way around this; it is the truth. But while I make no excuses for the companies that run them, the reality is that, while supplying ammunition to opponents and good stories for newspapers, these poorly managed operations represent only a small fraction of charter schools nationwide. Only about 3 percent of charter schools that operated in 2012–13 were not operating in 2014.[45] Of these, not all closed because of low academic performance. Some of them closed due to low enrollment and others closed over financial issues.[46]

Opponents, however, pounce on the few high-profile examples and then argue that the entire model is flawed. The truth is that there are bad actors in every sector, just as there are bad traditional public schools. At least in the charter world the bad actors are easier to remove. If a charter school does not live up to the terms of its charter, it is closed. "It's sort of characteristic of private enterprise. You have the poor performers and the system finds them and eliminates them," says William

Edgerly, former CEO of State Street Bank, who successfully pushed for the first charter schools in Massachusetts in the early 1990s. However, he adds, "If you were talking about a public entity, there can be non-performers and it's a lot harder to do anything about them."

The truth is that charter schools—and especially ones managed by for-profits—are besieged all of the time. Overcoming the hurdles and roadblocks created by adversaries is a daily battle for education providers. So is dealing with the constant legislative and regulatory tinkering of some lawmakers and district officials, which often undercut charter schools and sometimes put education providers out of business altogether.

We nearly lost a school in Lowell, Massachusetts, in 2014 after the state Board of Elementary and Secondary Education changed the way it measured which school districts were the lowest performing. By adding a new metric based on performance growth to one that had previously looked only at state achievement scores, some big urban districts with large low-income populations no longer ranked in the bottom 10 percent and so no longer qualified for more charter schools. The new calculation, however, was flawed because better-off towns that already showed high academic performance would not show as much growth, while lower-performing districts, starting from a lower performance base, would obviously show higher growth.

The change undermined a law enacted in 2010 to double charter school enrollment in low-performing districts. But then suddenly, many of these big, troubled urban cities with large low-income populations were no longer eligible. These cities included Worcester, Brockton, Lawrence (a city whose school district was in state receivership at the time because of chronic underperformance), and Lowell, Massachusetts—all pulled off the list of qualifying districts and replaced by smaller, often more affluent towns such as Yarmouth and Dennis on Cape Cod.

Many consider the legislation a bad joke. Brockton, for example, was no longer eligible for charter schools because 43 percent of students had become proficient in English Language Arts and math, up from 42 percent in the previous year.[47] Jim Stergios, of the Boston-based think tank Pioneer Institute, viewed the move as "a de facto moratorium on charter school expansion," calling it a "newfangled way to establish yet another barrier to entry for charter schools."

The new rule could have shut our Lowell school, where we were in our second year of operation and the board was in the midst of financing and developing a new facility. The charter had permitted the school to take 1,200 students in grades kindergarten through 12, but because Lowell no longer fell in the bottom 10 percent, according to the new formula, our school would now only be permitted to have 350 students. The new rule would have essentially bankrupted the school as it could only expand to grade 4. "Without insulting anyone, I don't think most of these people understood what they voted on, or its impact on charter schools," says Pellegrino, the former Springfield city council member who had helped us with our first charter and was helping with the new facility for the Lowell school.

If I get a charter, and it says I can go for the first five years of my charter from 200 kids to 700 kids, and then you change it in year two, and say I can only go potentially to 400 kids, but it might change the next year and let me go to 500, or the next year and go back to 300... You might as well shut my doors.

As you can imagine, it is nearly impossible to line up financing, much less plan for the future, with this kind of instability. In the end, we had to hire lobbyists to explain the issue to lawmakers. Fortunately, they passed an exemption for existing schools so that we could continue as planned. But it was a close call. It is not surprising so many for-profit companies want less and less to do with this business.

While most entrepreneurs like a good challenge, few welcome entering markets, like the charter school one, which are so inhospitable to them. For-profits are forever being stigmatized in the sector, and making matters worse is the fact that many people buy into the baseless, yet politically catchy claim that for-profit companies are in it for the cash and not for the kids. Rarely are our opponents asked to prove it, or explain what they mean. If they were, they would have a hard time. The insinuation is that profits will come before, or even at the expense of, student success. The part that adversaries fail to mention is that because profits are on the line, for-profit-run schools have no choice but to be responsive to parents and to deliver high student achievement.

Further undermining for-profit companies is a general sense among the American population that for-profits have no business running public schools. Again, there is no logical basis for the belief. "People have been brainwashed to think that education should not be for-profit," says Leila Saad, a third-generation leader of SABIS, who has been in the education business for more than sixty years. "If asked why, they would realize there is no rational defense to support that line of thought."

For all of the disparaging talk about for-profit education providers, there has been little serious analysis of the different operating behaviors, management styles, spending patterns, or advantages or disadvantages of for-profits versus nonprofits. Here I would like to briefly explain the main difference between for-profit and nonprofit education providers. It largely boils down to taxation. With for-profits, any profits (defined as revenues less expenses) are taxed at the local, state, and federal levels; the remaining profits go to the shareholders. Nonprofits, by contrast, are not taxed and any profits remain with the nonprofit itself, as there are no shareholders. In the end, the SABIS U.S. charter model, in which profits do not go to shareholders but remain on the boards' accounts, is virtually indistinguishable from a nonprofit model. That said, I wholeheartedly support a for-profit model in which profits go to the shareholders. By rewarding shareholders, they are more likely to invest more money so that education providers can expand their school networks and help more kids.

Opponents of for-profits often try to draw other contrasts between the two models. They claim that nonprofits are more likely to take a higher-minded approach to education, not cut corners, and attract equally high-minded employees to teach—implying that for-profit schools only attract people interested in making money. "These distinctions are artificial," says Tom Pritchard of KIPP Metro Atlanta in Georgia. He adds, "In fact, the two models are basically similar. Both must have good outcomes if they are to survive, and both must consistently generate profit, whether taxed or untaxed, if they are to continue operating."

Ultimately, it is performance that counts. Leaders of for-profit hospitals, for example, are not forever being hounded over their tax status or what they are doing with their profits. What matters is whether the hospitals save lives. Not to sound melodramatic, but we too are in the business of saving lives—the lives of kids trapped in failing public schools.

Of great concern to companies like SABIS is the fact that ill-founded arguments about the perceived greed of for-profit operators, unfortunately, work with some lawmakers. Every year, state legislators somewhere are debating whether to ban for-profit education operators. As of April 2015, seven states restricted or banned for-profit companies from managing public schools. Some state bans, New York's for example, apply only to new charters, while other states, like Maine, only prohibit for-profit virtual charter schools (those that operate online). As of May 2015, charter school laws in five states (Mississippi, New Mexico, Rhode Island, Tennessee, and Washington) allowed charter school governing bodies to contract *only* with nonprofit management companies.

Some states, like Tennessee, carry this prohibition even though the state is having serious trouble recruiting education management companies of any stripe to its troubled sector, says Kerwin, president of the Center for Education Reform. The legislators' anti-for-profit stance often boils down to a fear of controversy, she says.

> *Legislators will say:* "Well, we have a lot of good nonprofits here, so we're O.K. And for-profits are just too controversial." *My response to them is:* "I don't think you understand the capital and investments that these for-profit entities bring. They're opening up schools and creating jobs in our most depressed neighborhoods."

So, where do all of these bans, hurdles, and roadblocks leave us? The education sector, which many people had hoped would grow more competitive and innovative, is totally unattractive to most entrepreneurs and doomed to fail unless leaders get smart about creating more productive policies.

Things have become so grim that former Secretary of State Condoleezza Rice has called the reality of so many "poor black kids trapped in failing neighborhood schools" the "biggest race problem of today." During an interview on Fox News in late 2014, she said: "That's the biggest civil rights issue of today. Anybody who isn't in favor of school choice, anybody who isn't in favor of educational reform, anybody who defends the status quo in the educational system, that's racist to me."[48]

Kenneth Campbell, a founding board member of the Black Alliance for Educational Options, says he finds troubling, and sadly ironic, the fact that the people most vehemently opposed to school choice rarely have children in failing schools:

> *It is offensive to me that many of the people who have this view would never put their kids in the same schools that they want other kids to be forced to stay in. Most of the time, the people who are making these arguments have options. They are people whose kids go to private schools, who live in the suburbs, or whose kids go to magnet schools. But I don't recall ever hearing a parent of a child who was attending a failing school say: "Well, no, we shouldn't have any other options. We're just going to ride this out and see what happens."*

CHAPTER 4

Success by the numbers

GIVEN THE MANY CHALLENGES this sector faces, you might rightly ask why entrepreneurs bother at all. Partly (and here I am speaking for SABIS) it is because we are passionate about education; and partly it is because there has been some progress. In this chapter I would like to share with you data that prove that school choice is working—and working extremely well for those students who need it most.

Of course, like everything associated with this controversial reform, the results of studies on charter school success and failure are often manipulated to prove particular points and support whatever case the person is making. There is also a lot of data out there of uneven quality. I would like to cut to the chase and share numbers from just a handful of the most reputable studies, and make only a few key points.

The first is this: Reform takes time. It is unrealistic to expect that an education organization will take over a public school, or start a new one from scratch, and that its students will outperform their peers at traditional public schools right away. It can happen, and some charter schools produce amazing results from day one, but it is unrealistic to expect it.

It takes time for students and teachers to adjust to their new environment. Some students come from schools where coasting from grade to grade with minimal learning is considered cool by peers and inevitable by teachers. Then they arrive at a school like ours, with a strong culture of learning, and see that excelling academically is the thing that is cool. Shifting mindsets does not happen overnight. In addition, it takes time for charter school teachers to bring so many students from underperforming schools up to grade level.

The next point is that not all charter schools are equal, just as not all public or private schools are equal. Some states and districts have charter schools that are performing off the charts with students' academic achievement growth in math and reading far surpassing their peers at traditional public schools by anywhere from seven to more than 100 days of learning per year.[1] Meanwhile, there are states and schools where students are not, on average, performing better than their peers at traditional public schools. I'll talk about why that might be later in this chapter.

Two things are clear from the data, however, and this is why I say the reform is working. First, charter schools are improving over time. I should add that partly aiding that trend is that bad charter schools are being closed—unlike bad traditional public schools, which can get bailed out and continue to fail students. Second, and significantly, students most in need of better schools are, on average, far better off at charter schools.

Charter school opponents tend to gloss over this fact. They prefer to peddle the notion that charter schools overall fare about the same as traditional public schools. And indeed, there is some truth to this statement. The reason is that when you look at average performance numbers across the country, you will find that students with less ground to make up, such as white and Asian students, and those from non-urban environments, tend not to benefit as much from charter schools; some actually do worse. What charter school adversaries fail to highlight, however, is that students from inner cities and from low-income families—and particularly low-income black and Hispanic students and English Language Learners—show big achievement gains at charter schools.[2] This is important because charter schools disproportionately serve these very same disadvantaged groups.

Here is a snapshot of charter school demographics from the 2013 National Charter School Study by the Center for Research on Education Outcomes (CREDO) at Stanford University.[3]

	All US public	US charters	27 state charters
Number of schools	99,749	5,274	5,068
Total number of students enrolled	49,177,617	1,787,466	1,704,418
Students in poverty	48%	53%	54%
English Language Learners	6%	N/A	9%
Special education students	13%	N/A	8%
White students	52%	36%	35%
Black students	16%	29%	29%
Hispanic students	23%	27%	28%
Asian/Pacific Islander students	5%	3%	3%
Other students	4%	4%	4%

N/A indicates data are not available at this level of disaggregation for this student group.
Source: Cremata et al., *National Charter School Study 2013*.

Figure 4.1 Demographic comparison of students in all U.S. public schools, U.S. charter schools, and charters in 27 states, 2010–11

Conventional wisdom

Adam Ozimek, an economist at Moody's Analytics, wrote in a January 2015 *Forbes* article titled "The Unappreciated Success of Charter Schools" that people should pay more attention to the fact that, on average, charter schools do a better job of educating disadvantaged students:[4]

> *I think the conventional wisdom on charter school evidence could be summed up thusly: "Some charter schools appear to do very well, but on average charters do no better and no worse than public schools."*
>
> *But I would like to propose a better conventional wisdom: "Some charter schools appear to do very well, and on average charters do better at educating poor students and black students." If the same evidence existed for some policy other than charter schools, I believe this would be the conventional wisdom.*

Despite the evidence, critics continue to claim that charter schools "cream the best crop" of students. This simply is not true. A 2014 review of empirical evidence by researchers at the University of Maine concluded that "a majority of students enrolled in charter schools are not the higher performing students. Quite to the contrary, they are more likely to be minorities and children living in poverty, and some have special needs or English language challenges."[5] As you can imagine, because charter schools typically enroll a higher percentage of academically underperforming students than traditional public schools, our work is extremely challenging.[6]

The last point I would like to make is that if charter schools performed highly overall but failed to benefit low-income or black students, opponents would be screaming about inequality and racism. Ozimek said as much in his January 2015 article in *Forbes*:

> *I'm not accusing anyone of conscious bias here, but I think if the empirical research on any other policy showed similar results that charters do for poor students and black students it would be far more widely embraced, and the average effects would be downplayed as less important.*[7]

And now for some data.

The largest study over time of the charter school sector, and the one most people agree is valid, is the National Charter School Study by CREDO. This study confirms two key things: First, that performance over time is improving at charter schools, as all charter school students showed significant progress since the previous CREDO study in 2009; and second, that disadvantaged students, including low-income black and Hispanic students as well as English Language Learners, benefit the most and are making big academic gains by attending charter schools.[8]

Here are some highlights taken from the most recent 2013 CREDO study of 27 states:

- On average, students attending charter schools have eight additional days of learning in reading and the same days of learning in math per year compared to their peers in traditional public schools.

- In both subjects, the trend since 2009 is on an upward trajectory, with the relative performance of the charter sector improving each year.

■ Related results for different student groups indicate that black students, students in poverty, and English Language Learners benefit from attending charter schools.

The key results are shown below, but first a little explanation. The CREDO study compares achievement test results of charter school students with those of their peers at traditional public schools. The comparison is expressed in terms of days of learning gained or lost. So, for example, +7 means that charter school students are seven days of learning ahead of their peers at traditional public schools.[9]

Look at how different groups of charter students fared compared with their peers at traditional public schools in reading and math in 2009 and in 2013:[10]

Student groups	2009	2013
Black (reading)	−7	+7
Black (math)	−7	0
Hispanic (reading)	−14	−7
Hispanic (math)	−14	−7
Low-income (reading)	+7	+14
Low-income (math)	+7	+22
English Language Learners (reading)	+36	+43
English Language Learners (math)	+22	+36

Table 4.1 Charter students compared with their peers at traditional public schools in reading and math in 2009 and in 2013

The main takeaway from these numbers is that the biggest and most obvious winners from charter schools are those students most in need, such as low-income students and

English Language Learners, and the benefits to them are significant. In a country where nearly one in three students from low-income homes fails to graduate on time, if at all,[11] those lucky enough to attend charter schools are making incredible strides. Low-income black students on average are picking up an astonishing 36 days of additional learning at charter schools compared with their non-charter school peers, while their Hispanic counterparts at charter schools are picking up 22 more days. Given these results, you would think that policy makers would do all they could to figure out why this is so and try to replicate it.

Student groups	2009	2013
Black low-income	+29	+36
Hispanic low-income	+14	+22

Table 4.2 Learning days gained by low-income groups, 2009 and 2013[12]

I would like to make one more point about the CREDO data. Over time, all students are doing better at charter schools. In reading, charter school students, on average, now significantly outperform their traditional public school peers. Looking at the 16 states first analyzed in 2009,[13] charter school students, on average, now gain eight days of learning each year in reading over traditional public school peers compared with a loss of seven days each year in the 2009 report. Students at traditional public schools still outperform charter school students in math, but the study shows that steady progress has been made over the past five years, and the learning deficit is now a third of what it was in 2009. With more time and legislative support for the reform to fully flourish, gains could be so much greater.

I mentioned earlier that performance is uneven and depends on the state and the school, and I would like to say again here: School choice is not a magic wand. Some charter schools perform better than others, just as some traditional public schools do—while some states and districts have better performing education sectors than others.

Still, empirical studies suggest that charter schools in many states are making a significant difference to the lives of their students. A 2013 study by researchers at the Massachusetts Institute of Technology showed compelling evidence on charter effectiveness, with significant gains in the Massachusetts Comprehensive Assessment System (MCAS), a standards-based state exam, Advanced Placement, and SAT scores for high school students attending Boston charter schools.[14] The report also noted that "students from charter high schools are more likely to attend four-year rather than two-year colleges, which means that they will be better prepared for jobs in a competitive innovation economy."[15]

Figures 4.2 and 4.3 (see pages 81 and 82) come from the report.[16]

Another widely cited and reputable study, by a Stanford University economist, found that students who entered lotteries and won places in New York City charter schools outperformed on state exams those students who failed to get places in the city's charter schools and remained at traditional public schools. The study also found that, on average, a student who attended a Harlem charter school for every grade between kindergarten and grade 8 would close about 86 percent of the achievement gap in math and 66 percent of the achievement

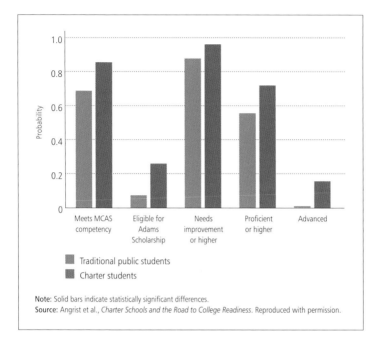

Note: Solid bars indicate statistically significant differences.
Source: Angrist et al., *Charter Schools and the Road to College Readiness*. Reproduced with permission.

Figure 4.2 Competency and MCAS categories: lottery estimates of the effects of Boston charter attendance

gap in English between these Harlem charter school students and those at traditional public schools in one of New York City's most affluent suburbs.[17, 18]

Not surprisingly, there has been a lot of attention paid to New Orleans, where only a handful of traditional public schools remain. The rest are now charter schools, which have been incredibly effective overall at boosting student achievement.[19] Before Hurricane Katrina decimated New Orleans and most of its schools, the graduation rate was about 50 percent and an estimated 64 percent of students went to schools designated as "failing."[20] Today, high school graduation rates have

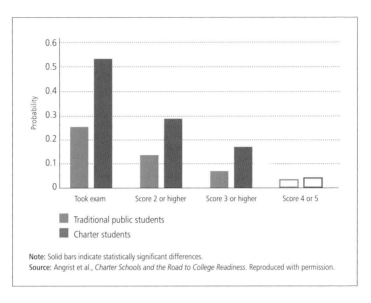

Figure 4.3 AP test taking and exam scores: lottery estimates of the effects of Boston charter attendance

increased by more than 20 percentage points to more than 70 percent, and the percentage of students attending failing schools is less than 10 percent.[21] (See Figure 4.4 opposite.)

Of course, there are other state analyses that show far less progress, if any. That is why I would like to draw your attention to which states seem to perform better and why that might be.

Todd Ziebarth of the National Alliance for Public Charter Schools (NAPCS) issues an annual report analyzing charter school laws and procedures by state. He says that, not surprisingly, states with rules and regulations conducive to fostering a healthy charter school sector often have better charter schools. Lawmakers have continued to make some progress, despite pushback from opponents. Even in 2014, with midterm elections and many gubernatorial races—with pro-charter

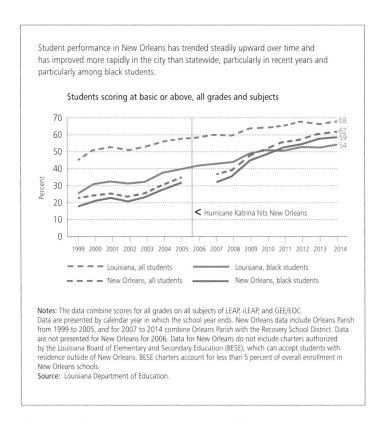

Student performance in New Orleans has trended steadily upward over time and has improved more rapidly in the city than statewide, particularly in recent years and particularly among black students.

Students scoring at basic or above, all grades and subjects

◄ Hurricane Katrina hits New Orleans

- - - Louisiana, all students ——— Louisiana, black students
- - - New Orleans, all students ——— New Orleans, black students

Notes: The data combine scores for all grades on all subjects of LEAP, iLEAP, and GEE/EOC.
Data are presented by calendar year in which the school year ends. New Orleans data include Orleans Parish from 1999 to 2005, and for 2007 to 2014 combine Orleans Parish with the Recovery School District. Data are not presented for New Orleans for 2006. Data for New Orleans do not include charters authorized by the Louisiana Board of Elementary and Secondary Education (BESE), which can accept students with residence outside of New Orleans schools. BESE charters account for less than 5 percent of overall enrollment in New Orleans schools.
Source: Louisiana Department of Education.

Figure 4.4 Closing the gap with charter schools[22]

lawmakers failing to support pro-charter bills and others introducing anti-charter bills—legislators in some states lifted caps that restricted growth, improved quality controls to encourage the opening and growth of better schools, and provided additional money to decrease funding gaps between charter schools and traditional public schools.[23] Better policies like these directly correlate to better performing charter schools. "We are pleased to see this relationship, obviously," says Ziebarth.

It is probably no coincidence that some places listed in the top ten of the NAPCS state law rankings, such as Louisiana and Washington, D.C.,[24] also score highly in the CREDO study when it comes to increasing student academic achievement at charter schools.[25] Louisiana, which ranked second in 2015 on the law rankings, for example, and allows a variety of charter school operators, including for-profits, has no cap on the number of schools, uses multiple authorizers, and has a transparent charter application, review, and decision-making process,[26] also boasts students at charter schools who are performing far better than their peers at traditional public schools.[27] The average one-year impact on academic growth from attending a charter school in Louisiana is 50 more days of reading and 65 more days of math learning.[28]

Washington, D.C., which allows a variety of charter school operators, including for-profits, ranked ninth in 2015 on the NAPCS law rankings of states with charter school-friendly policies.[29] Students at charter schools there have shown an astonishing 72 additional days of reading and 101 more days of math.[30]

My final point is this: If the genuine aim is to have consistently successful charter schools across the country, then legislators must create and enforce consistent and fair policies that attract great entrepreneurial talent, representing both for-profits and nonprofits, and that help the best schools to flourish.

CHAPTER 5

Politics and power plays

THERE ARE MANY GOOD REASONS why top entrepreneurial talent—particularly those running for-profit companies—typically steer clear of the charter school sector. Chief among them is that past success is no guarantee of future participation. Here is an example. Back in 2008, SABIS applied for a charter in Brockton, Massachusetts, a district ranked among the worst performing in the state. We had reason to be hopeful that our charter would be approved. At the time, SABIS ran two successful schools in Massachusetts, both boasting enviable records at closing the achievement gaps between students from high- and low-income families and between white and minority students. In fact, our minority students were outperforming their peers statewide. We imagined our record would be persuasive, particularly in a large minority district like Brockton.

The SABIS proposal—hundreds of pages long, explaining our curriculum, financials, and detailed education and management plans—was vetted by Department of Education professionals and then recommended for approval by the commissioner of education to the state Board of Elementary and Secondary Education, the state's sole authorizing body.

There was another reason for our optimism. Until then, this state board had always approved charters recommended by the commissioner of education. But not this time. Instead, our application was rejected, not on merit, but because of politics and officials who did not want district money going to a charter school. How do I know this? Because during a public panel discussion a few years later, the man who had been superintendent of Brockton Public Schools in 2008 said so.

When the panel's moderator, James Peyser, now Massachusetts's secretary of education, asked former Brockton Superintendent Basan Nembirkow why SABIS's Brockton application had little support given the success of its Springfield school, he replied:[1]

> Basically, the issue was finance and politics. It had nothing to do, or very little to do with the quality of the [SABIS] program. When SABIS came [to Brockton] we saw it as a financial threat. Simply as a financial threat. It took money away from us, which was about $4 to $5 million. Based upon that, our progress in BPS [Brockton Public Schools] would have been substantially affected. So my job defending the Brockton Public Schools, as the superintendent, was to do whatever I could to stop that particular threat at that time, so we mounted a very good political campaign.

Nembirkow says he personally believes that parents should have more choice about where their kids attend school and has personally spent the better part of his career creating alternatives to traditional public schools, but explains: "You tend to put aside your personal and philosophical leanings to do your job."[2]

Airing this story may sound like sour grapes, but I share it to highlight not just that the system is unfair and scares off good entrepreneurs, but that it is also unfair to children. Children should not be denied good schools over politics or because people running public school districts view competing charter schools as a "financial threat." Yet it happens all the time.

"It's all about the money; that's what it is," says Jack Brennan, a Boston lawyer, former Massachusetts state senator, and lobbyist who has worked with us over the years. "We hear it all the time when meeting with legislators when we're advocating on behalf of clients. They say: 'You know, I don't have a problem with charter schools. In fact, I kind of like charter schools. It's the money.'"

As I said earlier, the money does not belong to the districts. It travels with the students and belongs to them. In some states, such as Massachusetts, there is a generous reimbursement program that compensates districts at 100 percent the first year a student switches to a charter school and at a reduced percentage over the next five years, totaling 225 percent over six years.

We have since reapplied for a charter in Brockton, as well as for others in the state, only to be rebuffed in the same manner and for the same political and financial reasons. In one case, we were told that we were not a "proven provider" (an ill-defined and arbitrary clause added by former Governor Deval Patrick's administration that gave officials more power to deny applications) even though we have been operating award-winning schools in the state since 1995, all of which have long waiting lists.

After the second rejection in Brockton, some state representatives, perhaps fearing that we might return a third time, proposed a measure to prohibit for-profit companies from managing charter schools in the state. There is no way to read this legislative maneuver other than as a direct attack against SABIS, given that we are the only for-profit education management organization left in Massachusetts and the petition came from two local Brockton politicians who oppose school choice. The measure did not pass, but keeps resurfacing and is a constant thorn in our side.

Even the liberal-leaning *Boston Globe* supported our second application for a charter in Brockton by publishing a staff editorial in 2012, which argued that SABIS had earned the right, thanks to the exceptional achievement records of its other Massachusetts schools, to expand in the state, but for political reasons had so far been denied the opportunity to run other schools.[3]

The editorial, titled "Proving Themselves by Performing," read:

> *In 2008, an excellent SABIS proposal in Brockton was beaten back by powerful local politicians who didn't relish competing with charter schools for students and resources.*

The story concluded by saying that the education commissioner should put the needs of urban students first and rise above local school board politics to give SABIS a chance. You will not be surprised to hear that, in the end, the commissioner did not rise above politics, or put the kids first, and the charter proposal was denied.

Most people have heard the saying that "politics is local," but perhaps nowhere is this truer than in the battle over school choice. Presidents Bill Clinton, George W. Bush, and Barack Obama—all with their very different political views—generally supported charter schools and also had congressional backing.

Photo 5.1 A charter school student listening to Colorado's then governor discuss legislation related to the charter school authorization process.

Source: Photo by Andy Cross/*Denver Post*/Getty. Reproduced with permission.

But when you get down to the state and local levels, regardless of party affiliation, this support usually dissipates. What is right for the children no longer seems like the main issue. Sadly, as with so many things in life, what appears to matter most is money. Local district officials do not want to share funding with charter schools, so the students' needs take a back seat.

Influencing some state and local officials are the teachers unions with their massive memberships and equally massive buckets of money. The education sector employs more unionized staff than any other profession in America's public or private sector.[4] The most powerful teachers union in the U.S. is the National Education Association (NEA). It is the nation's largest union with 3.2 million members.[5] Annual spending by this organization on political candidates, political parties, and lobbying efforts is enormous. In 2014, for example, the NEA contributed close to $30 million to federal candidates, parties, political action committees (including Super PACs), and other politically active nonprofits, ranking third overall on an annual listing of large political donors[6] by the Center for Responsive Politics, a nonprofit, non-partisan Washington, D.C.-based organization. This figure does not include money spent supporting local politicians or time volunteered by union members to support various campaigns and causes.

The NEA has twice as many members as the country's second biggest teachers union, the American Federation of Teachers (AFT), which has 1.6 million members.[7] In 2014, the AFT spent nearly $20 million supporting federal candidates, parties, political action committees, and paying for lobbying efforts, and ranked seventh overall on the Center for Responsive Politics listing.[8]

In fact, over the past 25 years, the NEA ranked fourth on a list of top all-time "heavy hitters" (defined by the Center for Responsive Politics as groups that lobby and spend heavily), with large sums sent to candidates, parties, and leadership PACs between 1989 and 2014.[9] The AFT ranked sixth.[10] By comparison, the Teamsters Union came in 22nd, Citigroup (recipient of the largest government bailout of a single company in U.S. history)[11] ranked 27th, and Exxon Mobil was 96th out of 100.[12] Is it any wonder that politicians supported by teachers unions tend to do their bidding?

When we first applied for a charter in Brockton, Massachusetts, a new governor had come to power the year before. This was Deval Patrick, a Democrat, who was governor of Massachusetts until January 2015. Patrick replaced Republican Governor Mitt Romney who had supported the expansion of charter schools. Patrick, however, was more of a union man.

Labor unions spent $4 million dollars in the final weeks of Patrick's campaign to get him elected, according to the *Boston Globe*,[13] while the Massachusetts Teachers Association reportedly spent more than $2 million on a television ad campaign alone.[14] Still, education reformers had high hopes when they first met Patrick.

Jamie Gass of the Pioneer Institute, who has been involved in education reform for more than two decades, says that Patrick's staff at the time reached out to his think tank (more so than any other candidate), asked for their research, and genuinely seemed open to the best ideas, no matter where they originated. But things soon changed. "I think probably some time after he got the nomination, it became clearer and clearer that to really move forward both as a candidate, but also to govern, he had to have an enormous amount of support from the teachers union," explains Gass.

Soon after coming to office in 2007, Patrick began to reverse progress made in Massachusetts on education reform and charter schools.[15] Early on, he pushed for more executive authority over education policy. Under previous governors, the education commissioner was hired by the state Board of Elementary and Secondary Education, which fiercely guarded its independence from political interference from the executive branch.[16] In 2008, Patrick centralized governance of education policy by getting lawmakers to create a new cabinet-level secretary of education position to oversee a newly created Executive Office of Education, with the new education secretary getting approval authority over the hiring of commissioners of three education boards. Now, the commissioner of education would report to the secretary of education, who would report to the governor. While the commissioner of education would still technically report to the state board of education, this body no longer had the same autonomy because the governor and his secretary of education now had significant bureaucratic and budgetary authority over the board.

Next, Governor Patrick packed the state Board of Elementary and Secondary Education, the sole authorizing body for charters in the state, with people who were generally hostile to charter schools. Indeed, Patrick's first appointment to the board was Ruth Kaplan, a vocal critic of charter schools, who was closely aligned with the teachers association.

The following year saw increased political interference in Massachusetts's charter school authorization process, according to the Pioneer Institute. In one highly publicized example, the secretary of education sent a midnight email urging the education commissioner to approve a Gloucester charter school for political reasons, even though the department tasked with checking the organization's suitability found it deficient.[17, 18] The commissioner later claimed he had performed his own independent review of the application. But a Superior Court judge disagreed, finding "a strong factual showing that the commissioner, despite his affidavit to the contrary, did not perform his own evaluation of the GCA [Gloucester Community Arts] application but, to the contrary, ignored the state regulations and caved in to political pressure," according to an article by Charles Chieppo and Jamie Gass of the Pioneer Institute.[19] The Gloucester charter school was approved, but later closed owing to poor performance.

Patrick also shut down the Office of Educational Quality and Accountability (EQA), which exhaustively audited and assessed student performance, school financial numbers, and governance procedures—or, in short, held traditional public schools accountable. He called this office, which had been viewed as a model accountability system for other states, redundant. That was not the case, says Gass. "Governor Patrick got rid of EQA because superintendents, school committees and unions didn't like the scrutiny," he explains. "It was clear where the money was going and how the students were performing. It was really an education audit for districts and a counterbalance to charter school accountability." The end result was that it took the pressure off school districts to perform.

Ironically, it was under Patrick that the cap on charter schools was raised, and as a result, 16 new charter schools were approved. It is also worth noting that Massachusetts's officials had a powerful incentive to raise this cap, as doing so qualified the state for federal funding related to the Race to the Top grant program. In any event, it was not long after that the state Board of Elementary and Secondary Education changed the formula for measuring the progress of school districts, as explained earlier, thereby curbing future charter school growth in large urban communities that needed them most.

The editorial board of a local paper in Worcester, which was affected, wrote at the time:

> *Sadly, state education officials have made it clear they are more interested in protecting the jobs of bureaucrats and teachers than in letting real choice and competition do for education what they do for every other consumer market.*[20]

In the end at least some people were grateful to Patrick for his education policies—if not the families with children in the state's failing schools. Some 9,000 NEA members honored

Patrick in 2014 at a national event in Colorado by presenting him with America's Greatest Education Governor award, calling him a "staunch advocate for working families and the labor movement."[21]

Massachusetts is not the only state where education policy is usually more about politics than it is about educating children. Take, for example, Florida, and former Republican Governor Charlie Crist, an early and prominent advocate of school choice. As a Florida state senator in the 1990s, Crist co-sponsored legislation to implement the state's first charter school bill. He argued at the time that parents knew best what their children needed and should be free to pick the best schools for them. But that was when Crist was a Republican.

In 2014, when he tried to win his old job back, this time as a Democrat, he had changed his mind about a few things. He said he was no longer a fan of charter schools, telling one reporter: "It seems to me that charter schools and some of these other options are becoming more profit centers than learning centers."[22]

Then, during the run-up to the gubernatorial election, he sided with teachers unions in their lawsuit to dismantle a major school choice program totaling hundreds of millions of dollars that supported some 70,000 mostly minority children from low-income families.[23] The lawsuit argued that districts lose money when public school students use scholarships to attend private schools, even though that funding comes from private taxpayers and is not destined for state coffers.[24]

This school choice program was one that Crist himself had expanded when he was the state's Republican governor. "There's no partisan politics about kids," he had said in 2010 upon signing legislation for the expansion of this private K-12 scholarship program.[25] "It's all about doing what's right, first and foremost."[26] If only that were true.

As charter schools have gained traction, opponents have turned up the heat, and some of these battles can be remarkably petty and mean. In 2014, the Tennessee Charter School Center, an advocacy group, won approval for a new law allowing charter school operators denied locally to seek charter approval from a state authorizing board. Not long after, it was payback time. Four unions in Nashville, Tennessee, asked the Internal Revenue Service (IRS) commissioner to review the nonprofit tax status of the organization, arguing that the group had engaged in more lobbying than was legal for a nonprofit.[27] The advocacy group's small victory appears to have come at a price, and now it would have to spend time answering questions from the IRS. The CEO disclosed at the time that the nonprofit spends well below the 15 percent legal limit.[28]

The same year, 2014, was a particularly brutal one for charter school advocates in Illinois. Nearly a dozen union-pushed bills sought to limit where charter schools could be located, prohibit them from marketing themselves to students, and abolish a commission with the power to overrule local school boards and grant charter licenses.[29] Andrew Broy, president of the Illinois Network of Charter Schools, called the year the "worst [legislative] session for charter schools in the history of Illinois" and said passage of these bills could be the "death knell" for charter expansion.[30] "These bills ... weaken the communities that charter schools serve, which, in Illinois, are mainly African-American and Latino," he said.[31]

Perhaps no story better illustrates how bitter and personal these battles over charter schools can get—and how little they really are about the kids—than what has been going on in New York in recent years. The story starts with Mayor Bill de Blasio, the same union-friendly mayor who had been questioned over the propriety of accepting a $350,000 donation for his political advocacy group from the United Federation of Teachers (which the *New York Times* identifies as "probably the most powerful organization in local Democratic politics")[32] amid contract talks with these same union officials.[33] The talks resulted in 2014 in a new nine-year $9 billion labor contract, which raised pay by 18 percent and included billions of dollars in back pay.[34]

Less than two months into office, de Blasio began to unwind his predecessor's school choice programs by cutting funding for charter school construction after 2015, calling for a "moratorium" on locating new charters inside existing city schools (in which they share space),[35] and then rescinding a promise made by his predecessor, Mayor Michael Bloomberg, to allow nine charter schools to share space with city-run public schools come autumn of 2014.[36]

In case there was any doubt that the move was both political and personal, de Blasio rescinded space-sharing arrangements for three schools run by a longtime political nemesis, Eva Moskowitz, leader of Success Academy Charter Schools and among the city's more prominent and vocal charter school advocates.

It turns out that de Blasio was keeping a campaign pledge made at a union-sponsored event the previous May at which he said: "It's time for Eva Moskowitz to stop having the run of the place ... She has to stop being tolerated, enabled, supported. There's no way in hell Eva Moskowitz should get free rent, O.K.?"[37]

Some 17,000 parents and teachers had already made it clear what they thought of de Blasio's anti-charter school proposals, which included charging rent to charter schools for government-owned space, when they marched across the Brooklyn Bridge to City Hall in October 2013, during his mayoral campaign.[38] Wearing t-shirts with the slogans "Charter Schools Are Public Schools" and "My Child, My Choice," parents vented their frustration.[39] "Bill de Blasio, he needs to calm down and give our kids a break," parent Sheila Snipes was quoted as saying. "It should be equal for everybody."[40]

A media blitz followed, with TV ads running dozens of times a day, with one featuring children's faces disappearing as a voiceover spoke of their lost hopes and opportunities with the loss of their schools.[41] The campaign struck a nerve and de Blasio's popularity ratings plunged, with 49 percent of voters expressing disapproval with his handling of the issue.[42]

Three months into office, de Blasio started backpedaling. He reversed his decision to block dozens of co-locations and vowed to find space for the Success Academy students.[43] Then, speaking at a church, the mayor admitted to making mistakes and promised in future to reach out to all children no matter what kinds of schools they attended. "They are all our children, they all deserve a solution," he said.[44]

Sadly, the solutions offered by the mayor fell short. In October 2014, some 20,000 kids, parents, and educators from charter schools publicly rallied against the mayor again, this time in a park in Lower Manhattan, saying that government-imposed limits on charter school expansion made no sense in the city, given so many failing public schools (see callout box). They called the mayor a hypocrite and said that if he were serious about ending inequality, he would be helping poor children trapped in failing schools.[45]

Where is the outrage?

New York public school students deserve a solution. Here is what Families for Excellent Schools, a grassroots organization of families of public school children, wrote in the introduction to a 2014 report on failing schools: [46]

> *If one-fourth of New York City subway trains were constantly and chronically late, the streets would simmer with rage. If diners at one-fourth of restaurants were greeted with severe health code violations, the panic would be overwhelming. And if one-fourth of police precincts let nine out of ten crimes go unsolved, would the President even hesitate to deploy the National Guard? Those hypothetical scenarios seem unthinkable. Yet at nearly one-fourth of public schools across New York City, more than 90 percent of students are being failed.*

It should be clear by now to anyone who truly cares about finding a solution to failing schools that a bipartisan, non-political approach is necessary. Of course, this is easier said than done. Even when politicians generally approve of charter schools, out of political expediency they tend to support them in ways that ruffle few feathers.

"There's too much pressure on politicians," says Harry Patrinos, practice manager in the World Bank's education sector. "You've got politicians who don't want to sound like they're saying the wrong thing, so that even when they do

New York's failing schools

Here are some alarming statistics on public schools in New York compiled by Families for Excellent Schools:[47]

More than 90 percent of students at nearly a quarter of New York City schools (the so-called "forgotten-fourth") cannot read or do math at grade level.

371 schools with some 143,000 students—roughly the same number of public school students in Seattle, Atlanta, and Sacramento combined—are affected by this failure.

Performance of both the elementary and middle schools in the "forgotten fourth" has declined since 2003.

Enrollment at these schools has plunged by 46 percent over the past ten years and continues to dramatically decline.

It's not just New York City ...

There are 203 severely failing schools outside of New York City, with more than 100,000 children trapped in these schools.

More than 400 school districts in New York State lack even one school where a majority of children meet academic standards.

Across Buffalo, Rochester, Syracuse, and Yonkers, six out of ten schools are failing 90 percent of their kids.

Children of color pay the highest price for the state's education crisis. One out of every five African-American and Hispanic children outside New York City attends a severely failing school, compared with one out of every 50 white and Asian children.

push for diversity and competition, they often limit participation to NGOs (non-governmental organizations) and not-for-profits. This is often for political reasons." Most steer clear of advocating a free market approach with full for-profit participation because it could look bad in headlines, adds Patrinos.

This is where they sell kids short. By playing politics and limiting the playing field to certain kinds of organizations, and then piling on top loads of restrictions that curb their ability to compete, politicians rob kids of genuinely competitive schools and undermine America's economic future.

CHAPTER 6

The case for a free market

WHEN I READ ABOUT CHARTER SCHOOLS and their supporters, I often find myself confused about whom exactly they are talking about. The media, at its worst, paints a portrait of right-wing libertarians and corporate high-flyers out to dismantle public education. They make it all seem so conspiratorial.

Sure, the Walton Family Foundation funds initiatives to back charter schools, as do other wealthy and successful people. However, most people pushing to give children equal access to good schools are ordinary folks by comparison. Take as examples the individuals on our charter school boards, many of whom have come to us unsolicited and have asked us to consider opening a school in their neighborhoods. These people represent a broad range of backgrounds and experiences far removed from the polarizing types of people portrayed in the press.

I would like to share two examples with you. Larry Chenault is a martial arts expert from New Jersey. Ten years ago he was running after-school and summer programs for children who wanted to learn martial arts. Chenault soon realized that the children he taught were way behind in school, so he applied for a No Child Left Behind grant and started tutoring them himself. He would throw in a free martial arts lesson afterwards.

He soon discovered that the guidelines, which permitted only a few weeks of tutoring, were not enough to help these children who lagged so far behind. At that point, he started researching other options and came across our company. Today, Chenault is part of the founding board for our school in Trenton, New Jersey.

Then there is Anne Kandilis, a former partner at a "Big Four" accounting firm. Her cousin was the chairman of the SABIS International Springfield school board. For years, he had asked her to join the board, but she was too busy. Then her niece, who had just finished her freshman year at our school, died of a brain aneurism. Kandilis's family created a scholarship program in their child's name, and so Anne attended the graduation ceremony to see the scholarships awarded. She said she was so impressed by the poise and accomplishments of the students that she immediately offered to get involved.

Later, while part of a community effort to rebuild a Springfield elementary school following its destruction by a tornado, she says she became aware of the troubling state of many local public schools:

> When I really started looking at the schools in Springfield, I thought, we are not educating our children effectively. For many of these children, education is their only way out of poverty. And yet, we're creating a legacy of poverty in our community. More than two-thirds of our schools in Springfield were classified as Level 3 or 4,[1] which is not proficient. You have many, many students who are scoring below proficient and who attend schools that are in the bottom percentage of schools in the state.

Kandilis eventually became an education policy fellow at the Rennie Center for Education Research & Policy and Northeastern University, as well as a strong supporter of school choice and for-profit involvement. She still serves on the board of our Springfield school.

So why do I tell you about these people? Because they are not hedge fund billionaires or members of the Walton family, but regular folk who care enough about the kids around them to try to make a difference. They do not have an agenda or anything financially at stake, like their own jobs. They see serious problems in public education, which they want fixed by the best people for the job.

Here is what Chenault has to say:

I'm for any organization—it could be a private school, it could be a Catholic school, it could be a for-profit school—as long as the child is mastering the essential concepts and moving forward and becoming a good citizen. I'm all for it. I don't care who it is, for-profit or not-for-profit, as long as the kids are excelling academically. That's where I stand.

With that thought in mind, I would like to turn to a subject that is clearly important to me: *Who* should fix these problems? Before I answer by saying, "Anyone and everyone who can make a difference," let me take a step back. The long-term goals of any education reform initiative should be to make lives better for children and to improve their futures. They ought to be about closing achievement gaps and ultimately about keeping the U.S. economically, culturally, and socially strong. But first and foremost, it should be about the kids.

Everyone loves to say this, but then politics and special interests take hold, and it is not about the kids—not at all. If it were, there would be clear, bipartisan political leadership to improve all forms of public schools, including charter schools. There would also be consensus that the best organizations, no matter what their tax status, should be allowed to help. This issue is far too big and too serious to shut out good participants.

To use a simple analogy, imagine a fire is burning across a city and yet fire fighters must use only a few of the hoses in their trucks and only a limited amount of the available water. Similarly, by closing the charter school sector to for-profits, as lawmakers in some states have done and others are considering, they are essentially trying to put out raging fires with too few hoses and very little water.

There is no rational argument for barring for-profits from the sector, says Basan Nembirkow, the longtime school superintendent in Massachusetts, who has sat on both sides of this debate. (He moved against charter schools when he served as school superintendent, such as in Brockton, as I explained in an earlier chapter, but says he supports school choice and has, in other jobs, helped develop different varieties of public schools.)

Nembirkow asserts:

The criticism against for-profits is that they make a profit, which is kind of interesting in a capitalist society. I find it kind of incongruous. When you talk to people, and you push them a little bit, you find out that they can't really tell you what their objections to for-profits are in a clearly articulated manner, outside of the fact that schools were always this way [meaning nonprofit run] and these people are coming in and they're making money off our kids. It's a visceral reaction rather than a rational one.

So, what are the rational reasons to have for-profits running charter schools? The answer essentially comes down to a handful of things: Accountability, sustainability, more competition (i.e., more hoses to put out raging fires), efficiency, professionalism, and innovation.

The first point that I would like to make is that profit is nothing to be ashamed of; it instills discipline and keeps companies accountable. A charter operator motivated by profit will also be motivated to treat teachers well and to ensure that students are learning and that facilities are maintained. Otherwise, teachers will quit, parents will send their children elsewhere, and the for-profit operator will lose money. The idea that for-profits are going to cut spending or use most of the money for marketing and then offer cheap, low-quality education is simplistic and naïve.

We cannot afford to sacrifice quality for profits or we will be out of business. You could easily argue that money is the very motivation that school leaders need to turn things around. Ralph Bistany of SABIS, who has been in the for-profit education business for sixty years, sums up the argument like this: "The owners of for-profit companies go to sleep at night thinking of ways of improving their product because otherwise they lose their shirt."

I am not saying that money is the only thing that motivates operators of for-profits. Our team is also driven by a desire to make the world a better place by educating kids. In the end, though, we are pragmatists and see that the best way to bring high quality education to a growing number of students is with a for-profit approach.

A successful for-profit approach requires constant growth. Yet even I sometimes ask myself: When is enough, enough?

We have schools in 16 countries on four continents; 15 of our schools are in the U.S. We could stop right now and be content to focus on the schools we currently manage. But in reality it does not work very well that way. By growing the business we improve it and this benefits our students. With each new school we add, we achieve better economies of scale across the network, and we use the money yielded from these efficiencies to help our students by bettering our product, such as by improving technologies and teaching methods. And we keep on building, so it is a continuous loop that feeds back into itself. Again, this approach hugely profits our students, and that is the point. So really, how could we stop?

And yes, money is a key motivator, but why should this be seen as a bad thing? Far from it, being money-focused is what drives for-profit schools to grow and thrive, remain efficient, be innovative, and guard against complacency. If your very existence depends on staying ahead of the competition, you cannot risk failing on any of these fronts.

Ultimately, it is money as a motivator that propels us to serve a greater good in public education. And while I do not mean to imply that nonprofits are by contrast more complacent, particularly inefficient, or lacking in innovative spirit, I am saying that when for-profits fail to be any of these things, they eventually go out of business.

The for-profit sector is absolutely vital to creating successful and sustainable schools that scale over time. The private sector generally has ready access to cash from public and private markets and so has an easier time building businesses that are more shock-resistant, sustainable, and scalable. This is less true of nonprofit charter management companies, whose financial viability is typically dependent on the goodwill of charitable contributors. Nonprofit operators must lean heavily on corporate and individual donors to keep cash coming in to acquire and refurbish their facilities, buy classroom equipment, and hire teachers. So yes, it is back to money again.

Better access to capital means that it is also generally easier for for-profits to open more than one school; with increased revenues and economies of scale, they eventually open more schools. Many people would agree that bigger chains of well-financed, sustainable public schools with uniformly high standards are better than lots of little mom-and-pop run schools of varying quality that are dependent on fundraising to survive.

I should say here that this entire scenario is dependent on having a charter school environment with clear regulations and a system that is fair for all education providers. Currently, this is not the case. The market I imagine in which money flows to the best performers—those schools with effective learning models and students performing to their highest potential—does not exist. This is because officials keep changing the rules.

It is not unusual to learn halfway through the school year, for example, that per pupil funding is going to be cut or that the school cannot have as many students as expected in the following year. Try telling that to private sector investors, and good luck getting their money. Ultimately, investors and companies, deterred by so many unknown variables and too much risk, take their money elsewhere, leaving the U.S. education sector in its current situation of limited access to hoses to put out too many raging fires.

Bigger chains of schools also bring another benefit: The increased professionalism that comes with expansion. "As businesses grow, they tend to develop more sophisticated internal systems," says Stergios of the Pioneer Institute, which has worked to improve the accounting policies and operation procedures of charter school operators. He says that for-profits—which may be fewer in number than nonprofit operators, but tend to run multiple schools—are better positioned to develop solid professional management. As their businesses grow, for-profit operators have to improve and standardize protocols and procedures, which often leads to greater transparency and better accounting policies. "You want to get these things right for the kids," he says, "and you want to get them right for the movement."

Certainly not all schools are professionally managed, and that is when government steps in. It is the government's job to hold operators to account by setting achievement standards, monitoring results, and making sure all schools meet these standards. However, this should be the full extent of government's role.

What a school does to meet or exceed standards, including how it uses its money, pays its teachers, or motivates them, is the school's business. An education provider might have a fantastic approach that gets kids to excel at all subjects by meditating each morning. What does government care as long as the provider can deliver results that far exceed their standards? And really, what does a legislator—or even a parent—care, as long as the school is producing lots of graduates who score well on state-wide exams and go on to college?

Most states require education providers to be overseen by a nonprofit board of directors, thereby adding another layer of bureaucracy and influence from people who do not necessarily have anything at stake. In the current system, any board member can decide on a whim that he or she wants the school to, say, integrate a pet theme of theirs into the curriculum or introduce a new disciplinary measure. While making changes requires majority approval by a board, one strong-willed individual can influence others to support a measure and, as things stand, there is not a whole lot the school management can do to stop it.

Ultimately, government should not force on school operators a governance structure that permits others to dictate how results should be reached. Rather, government should oversee results and hold schools accountable for achieving those results. Boards, if they must remain, should operate as they do in other industries. They should provide oversight and not have executive authority and be subject to independent review.

In the end, it is important to remember that the real benefits a free market brings to public education have not fully been realized. There has been some innovation—the original idea behind charter schools—related to the ways students' time is structured, how teachers teach, and how technology is used. These are all important things, but there could be so many more advances given freer competition.

As things stand, a truly competitive market for education has hardly been tested. For-profits are aggressively discouraged from entering it, which stands in stark contrast to other social sectors in which government welcomes for-profits to increase competition and innovation. More than twenty years on from the creation of the first charter schools, the for-profit segment represents a mere 13 percent of the charter school industry, which is predominantly (67 percent) made up of independent, nonprofit, single-site schools.[2] The remaining 20 percent of charter schools are run by nonprofit organizations that operate more than one school.[3]

Yet instead of encouraging for-profit operators to try to make a difference, lawmakers continually cave to special interest groups and keep shutting them out. Jamie Gass of the Pioneer Institute sums it up like this: "Public education has been remarkably resistant to market forces and it's because they [special interest groups] are really good at lobbying."

It is all extremely short-sighted, explains SABIS's Leila Saad:

> How can you judge something before you let it happen? We've seen the results of people who are given a chance really—not after one or two years or three years—and who are passionate about doing a good job, about building something worthwhile. Let them. Why should you stifle their ambition?

There will certainly be failures along the way—just as there have been failures in the traditional public school sector for decades—but if unfettered competition were encouraged and supported, the best companies would survive and mature, innovate, attract more students, and build more great schools.

Then again, this is our adversaries' real fear. It is not that we might fail or spend more money on marketing than on math books, or even that we might profit off of kids. What scares our adversaries most is that we will succeed where they have failed.

CHAPTER 7

When the stars are aligned

I BEGAN THIS BOOK BY telling you about our first charter school in Springfield, Massachusetts, which we opened more than twenty years ago. I told you about how we offered to take over the worst performing elementary school in the district but were soundly rejected by parents and community leaders out of fear and ignorance about our motives and teaching methods. I explained that instead we took over and turned around the second worst performing public elementary school in the district and how we expanded it to include a middle school and a high school. I then mentioned some successes we have enjoyed at this SABIS International Charter School (SICS), including a 100 percent college acceptance rate year after year for our graduates, and six silver medal finishes in a row on *U.S. News & World Report*'s "America's Best High Schools" listings.[1]

In the next two chapters, before I share some recommendations for the charter school sector, I would like to tell you the story of how our school in Springfield came about. I want you to better understand the challenges we faced and appreciate how we still managed to set up and run a successful school, and also introduce you to the very real people who made it possible.

Our school would never have existed at all if it were not for the fact that, in the early 1990s, leaders from opposing political parties joined forces to solve a serious problem in Massachusetts. An over-reliance on local property taxes had created a grossly unfair system in which kids in wealthy neighborhoods enjoyed beautiful public schools equipped with libraries and computers, while kids in poorer districts went without.

Key figures at the time, including a Republican governor, William Weld, two liberal Democrats and co-chairs of the education committee, Mark Roosevelt and Tom Birmingham, and also Democrats Tom Finneran, Massachusetts speaker of the House, and William Bulger, president of the State Senate, all agreed that fixing public education required greater accountability, high-stakes testing, and competition.

At the same time, influential business leaders such as William Edgerly, then CEO of State Street Bank, were lobbying politicians for better public schools. "We had a concern for the success of the city of Boston in various areas, economic and cultural," explains Edgerly. "And at the base of it had to be a successful public school system."

Edgerly and other business leaders felt that small measures were not enough. He recalls:

I began to realize that we were never going to get better schools unless we had significant change. Because the only thing that happened is that more money got thrown at the problem. The solution became reasonably clear in that it involved choice and accountability.

These people all contributed to the creation and passage of a sweeping education bill, the Education Reform Act of 1993, which called for a sharp increase in state funding for poorer districts in exchange for higher standards and better accountability. The bill also called for 25 charter schools.

The point here is that the charter school movement in Massachusetts got off to a strong start thanks to political support from lawmakers from both political parties and from concerned business leaders, all of whom were committed to making public schools better for kids. You might even say the stars were aligned in Massachusetts for serious education reform. How things played out locally is another story.

Springfield, a city 90 miles west of Boston, was the kind of place that Massachusetts lawmakers had in mind when they pushed for education reform. A once thriving industrial city, Springfield had lost its manufacturing sector and fallen on hard times. Unemployment was high, property taxes were low (resulting in less money for school districts), and public schools needed help.

While some kids managed to make it through Springfield's public schools and go to college, roughly one in seven in 1994 dropped out.[2] The situation was worse for minorities in the early 1990s, with dropout rates estimated as high as 45 percent for some groups, according to Peter Negroni, the Springfield school superintendent at the time.

Exacerbating matters was a system popular in the 1980s and early 1990s, bizarrely referred to as "social promotion," in which teachers would move students along to the next grade whether they had learned anything or not, ostensibly to keep them with their peers, but often simply to get them out of their classrooms. This left many students ill-prepared for the real world, much less ready for college. Now imagine the impact of those kids, along with the dropouts, on the social and economic wellbeing of a city.

At the time, few in Springfield saw school choice as something that might change things. Bob Markel did not think it would help, and that could have been a problem as he was Springfield's mayor. He says that back then he believed that children were products of their environment and a new type of public school was not going to change anything. As it turned out, he did not have much say in the matter.

Governor Weld visited his office in Springfield one day. "He sat me down and said, 'You're getting a charter school. Make the best of it,'" recalls Markel. "I said, 'O.K.,' even though I didn't know what a charter school was back then. I had no idea."

Convincing other local leaders proved more challenging. The one person pushing for school choice in Springfield was Negroni. Unlike most school superintendents, who viewed charter schools with skepticism, if not with outright hostility, Negroni, a longtime teacher and principal in the New York City public schools, thought of them as "lightning rods" for change. "I believed that we could take schools and make them examples of what schools could be," he explains. "And that when that happened, other schools would see the challenge and begin to work at being better schools."

Few people agreed with him; some did not even see the point of educating all students to a high standard. Negroni recalls explaining to community business leaders that while the city was educating about 40 percent of its students reasonably well, 60 percent were falling through the cracks. He told them that if he had his way, every kid in Springfield would get a private education and go on to college, to which one of those present replied: "Well, who's going to clean the beds in our hospitals and our floors?"

Overall, though, he says that the business community was supportive and helpful. This was not true of the teachers union, however, which was vehemently opposed to charter schools. Negroni characterizes his relationship with the union as an "on again and off again" one, depending on which change he was trying to make, but adds that "the charter school issue was huge and they were very angry with me."

As you can probably guess, reforming schools without union support is extremely challenging. Mayor Markel's successor, Michael Albano, remembers making various attempts, while in office in Springfield from 1995 to 2003, to lengthen the public school day and year to boost student achievement. Union officials played hardball every time, he says, demanding roughly 10 percent extra in pay per hour added, per teacher. So, two hours would mean 20 percent on top of teachers' salaries, which already totaled hundreds of millions of dollars, says Albano. "You do the math. Where are you going to get the money? You can't." In four terms in office, he eventually got 15 minutes more a day out of all of those contract negotiations, "and it wasn't cheap."

While there were many good public school teachers in Springfield, most changes were met with resistance. Negroni says that the resentment extended to a new professional development program he was running at the time, at which he recalls seeing some teachers reading newspapers during training sessions and watching others dump their materials in the trash after class. He approached one of those teachers and asked: "Why are you throwing this away?" to which the teacher replied: "Because it's worthless, just like everything else that you're doing here."

The irony was that many Springfield district teachers no longer even lived in the city and so their children did not attend Springfield public schools, says Markel. "Even the ones that lived in the city didn't put their kids in the public schools." Their only stake in the public system was their jobs, he adds.

Markel, a liberal Democrat, who had been elected with teacher union support and was a personal friend of the president of the teachers union, says he initially saw these friends and allies as the people who were going to advance education reform, but soon realized his mistake. "It took a while for me to understand that my allies were a big part of the problem," he says. "A lot of politicians get into office and they say, 'Oh hell, my friends are the problem.' And then what do you do?"

"I became gradually convinced that there were so many barriers to reform that while Negroni might be able to do it, it would take him a generation to get it done, chipping away," he adds.

The biggest sticking point is typically money. When students go to charter schools their funding goes with them, rather than to their sending districts. District officials do not like this, nor do most superintendents, including Springfield's current one (at the time of this book's publication in 2015), Daniel Warwick. He says that when you lose students, you lose their funding, but the district still needs to employ teachers, have classrooms, and pay the same overhead.

Markel, no longer mayor and so no longer subject to political pressures from both sides, sees things differently.

If you can't do the job, you're going to lose resources and eventually people get laid off, and eventually, we may have to close the school. If you want the resources back, improve your outcomes and the students will come back and you'll get the money back. This competition business makes a lot of sense to me. They [underperforming schools] ought to pay a price because I don't know of any other way to get them to change.

Fortunately, in our case Superintendent Negroni supported charter schools, but there were still many hurdles ahead. A big one involved getting our organization approved by the Springfield school committee. This would prove challenging, as the committee doubted the district even needed a charter school. "Here were these private companies going to try to educate kids that we had been trying to educate forever," recalls Beth Conway, then chair of a subcommittee within the school committee tasked with meeting prospective school management organizations. "I wouldn't say I had a very positive feeling."

Conway says the first company that pitched her committee promised a computer for every child, to which she told them: "We live in a poor urban district. Many of these kids don't have a place to sleep at night, much less a place to keep safe a computer." They did not get the committee's approval.

Representatives from SABIS met with the group next. Conway says she thought it would be a short meeting and a quick goodbye, but that is not what happened. Halfway through the meeting, SABIS's Ralph Bistany, who had remained silent up to then, leaned forward and said: "Mrs. Conway, what do you want to know about our school? Because I will tell you everything you want to know." Then he just started talking, recalls Conway, and she was mesmerized.

He went on for about two hours, talking about the school's methodology, and how English and math were the cornerstones of education. He focused on basics and explained what SABIS could deliver. "There were no bells and whistles," says Conway. "No computers going home. It was solid and went back to education basics and what the students needed." She was sold. This surprised her fellow committee members—and even more so when Conway agreed to help promote SABIS to local community leaders, including city councilors and influential business people.

Now it was time to get a school. Negroni's plan was for us to take over the worst performing elementary school in the district. He figured that in this way, if we were successful, no one could later argue that we had an unfair advantage because we took over a reasonably good school or built one from scratch. The DeBerry School ranked last among elementary schools in the district. You would have thought that given there was nowhere to go but up, parents and teachers would have welcomed us, or any solution, to turn around the failing school. That is not what happened.

The school had strong black community roots. Parents were skeptical of outsiders and supportive of the school's principal. "This is our school," was what people were saying, recalls Markel. "It's bad, but it's ours." Critics, including vocal union people, soon spread the word that SABIS was run by outsiders and implied that we would essentially be stealing money from poor Springfield kids.

After SABIS's first presentation to the school, it was obvious we were not welcome. Markel says a black minister from the community told him privately: "You're not bringing in a lot of white guys from Minnesota to take over our school." Negroni tried to convince people that SABIS provided private education all over the world and was offering it free to children in Springfield. But they wanted no part of it.

Faced with such fierce opposition, the school committee voted to switch to the Glickman School, the second worst performing elementary school in Springfield. Getting Glickman proved to be no picnic either, but by this point our company had a groundswell of support from parents who wanted a SABIS education for their children. The Glickman School got approval, and then it was on to the city council for their final O.K. (Negroni as superintendent had no control over school buildings and so required city approval to get one.)

The meeting in city council chambers at city hall was standing room only. The teachers union showed up with members and parents carrying signs. There was a lot of name-calling. We were called foreigners, thieves, even mobsters. For all of the emotion we provoked, you would think SABIS had come to recruit kids to dig ditches rather than to offer them a free, college-preparatory education. The council, by a 4 to 3 vote, gave us the green light.

That is when the real work began. We first hired a director. (We do not use the term "principal" because the leaders of our schools also oversee the business side of operations, including all budgetary items, hiring and firing, etc.) Michael Glickman (no relation to the school) had worked in public education for 27 years. He had been at some of the public meetings and liked what he heard from SABIS representatives. He says he felt ready for a change professionally. At one of those meetings, which had grown unruly, Glickman had asked people to give us a chance to talk and hear what we had to say.

Hiring teachers proved challenging. Teachers at the

Glickman School were told they could reapply for their jobs, but none did as this meant crossing the union, which had told the teachers it did not support charter schools and did not want them working for them. Mostly, we hired recent college graduates and teachers from parochial schools.

Some 300 of roughly 308 students stayed at the school, while another 150 children joined through a lottery system. The culture at the school had to change immediately. Fighting, cutting classes, and rudeness would not be tolerated. Glickman recalls running red duct tape down the center of the corridors and instructing the kids to walk on the right-hand side only. No longer could they walk six abreast, oblivious to the needs of others. "It's showing them that we're not going to put up with any nonsense," says Glickman. "They're here to work."

Beyond being told to shape up, the children were told that they were up to the challenge. Glickman says that early on they instituted a program in which 7th-graders—the highest grade we had in the first year before adding more in subsequent years—would at the end of each day escort kindergartners to their buses or to where parents were waiting. "We gave them responsibility," says Glickman. "It makes them feel that they're part of the program and they're helping out—even kids with discipline problems. One way to turn them around is to give them responsibility."

Despite progress at the school, or perhaps because of it, the unions turned up the heat. As I said earlier, the unions are extremely powerful. They donate money to political campaigns, and their members hold signs and volunteer to get out the vote. Union members also vote in high numbers and they talk to reporters. A lot.

Indeed, if your child is doing just fine at a public school or if you do not have children, then you might easily be persuaded by claims that charter schools like ours are not run in the best interest of children, when the reality is that the issue is not even about the children. It is about the adults.

"The union's job is to preserve the jobs and conditions for their workers as they always were, and make them a little bit better," explains Basan Nembirkow, the former Massachusetts school superintendent who dealt with union representatives daily. "They weren't worried about the kids," he says. "Unions are never worried about the kids. The union's job is to protect its clientele."

To protect its clientele (teachers), the union launched an aggressive campaign against us. From the beginning, there were talk radio shows with union members putting us down, and local newspaper stories, sometimes twice a week, making false claims, such as that our teachers were not real teachers, but rather teachers' aides. They said that we were keeping the money and not spending it on students and that we were using "secretive" class materials.

In the early days of the school's operation, we decided to reach out to the community to dispel some of these myths, and so we hosted an open house. We invited teachers from all of the district public schools and union leaders and took out an ad in the local paper to get other educators to come to the event. Our teachers prepared their coursework and brought out their books and their students' class work to share. They set up a computer to show the school's testing methods (we test students weekly to make sure they have mastered key concepts). They put out soft drinks and cookies. On the night of the event, only a handful of people showed up, including just two teachers from the Springfield school district. "It was all geared toward educators and almost nobody came," says Conway, the former Springfield school committee member who was by then an assistant director at the school. "It was really, really awful."

The irony, however, is that while almost none of the district's teachers showed up, the names of their children started appearing on our school's waiting list. "They wouldn't support us," says Conway, "but they wanted their children in our school. It was mind-blowing that you would see so many teachers' kids on our waiting list."

Mary Lynn Hunter was one of those students in the school's first seventh-grade class. Her mother was, and still is, a unionized teacher in one of Springfield's public schools. She sent Hunter and her three siblings to SICS. "She always said that she's a mother first and is going to do what she thinks is best for her children and their education," says Hunter, who now teaches at our Springfield school and is head of the English department.

Hunter says that in that first year she was largely surrounded by other children of educators or from families who were paying attention to education reform in Massachusetts. She recalls her first year at the school, saying the atmosphere was far calmer and less violent than at her previous school, where she recalls one student shoving a bookcase onto another student and then stabbing him in the face with a pencil.

Demand for our school grew. After just one year, 495 kids appeared on our waiting list. Two years later, we had more than 1,000 kids on the list. By 2000, we had more than 3,000 names on it.

What accounts for the huge demand? Our students were testing off the charts. After the first year, the Iowa Tests of

Basic Skills, which had previously ranked the Glickman School second to last among Springfield elementary schools, now showed our students outperforming students in the city of Springfield at every grade level.

It helped that we had made a huge push to bring the students up to speed, which resulted in big and nearly immediate changes. In 1995, our first school year, 38 percent of our students were performing at or above grade level in math. By the 1996–97 school year, 64 percent of our students were at or above that level. In English, only 44 percent were at or above grade level initially. By 1996–97, 69 percent of all students were at or above grade level.

The staff were on fire, and there was a lot of passion. "There was not a single staff absence until mid-April of that first year," says Maretta Thomsen, another former public school teacher who joined SICS early on and later became its director. "We saw this opportunity to change the lives of these kids," she says, "and prove this would be a success."

And that is the point, isn't it? To change kids' lives.

Thomsen tells the story of one particularly bright girl from a bad neighborhood. She showed promise early on and so, along with a handful of other kids, was chosen to attend the annual summer leadership training camp for student leaders from throughout the SABIS network. That year, the students went to Bath, England, free of charge. She returned a changed person, says Thomsen:

This is a girl who came from the kind of neighborhood where there were many shootings and many girls getting pregnant. She thought this was her future too. She went to England and she came back to me and she said, "I never realized what I could do with my life."

From that moment on, this student did nothing but study, says Thomsen. She took math in the summer. She stayed late after school to keep studying. The hard work paid off. She earned a full scholarship, including room and board, to Smith College, a prestigious all-female college in Massachusetts. In fact, all 46 students in the school's first graduating class were accepted at colleges and universities, including prestigious ones such as Harvard and Georgetown, and 11 got full tuition scholarships. Meanwhile, union people had been telling anyone who would listen that our school was not accredited and none of the students would go to college.

These were the early days, and since then more than 1,000 students have graduated from SICS, as of the 2014 school year, and every single one of them was offered a two- or four-year college place. We are also proud of our four-year graduation rate of 93 percent during the 2013–14 school year, which is remarkable given the Springfield district's four-year gradua- tion rate of just 62 percent. In fact, our graduation rate over the last nine years averages out to 95 percent, compared to a 55 percent graduation rate in the Springfield district for the same period.[3]

Here are a few more statistics: For a relatively small school, and one that focuses primarily on academics, we have won two state basketball championships. In 2015, our Model Congress team won the top "Outstanding Delegation Award" for a sixth year in a row, along with $170,000 in scholarship money from the event. Graduating classes from 2011 to 2014 received an average of $10 million in scholarship money each year; the $11.5 million they received in 2014 averaged out to more than $110,500 per graduate for college.

Meanwhile, the DeBerry School—the one where parents

and leaders blocked us back in 1995—remains among the poorest performing schools in the district. As I mentioned in the Introduction, DeBerry has been named a Level 4 school,[4] meaning it is among the lowest achieving and least improving schools in the state. In 2014, only 21 percent of its students performed at or above grade level in English Language Arts, while only 39 percent were at or above grade level in math.[5]

Here I want to be clear about something: I am not saying that charter schools are the only answer to all of these problems. There are excellent and committed leaders in the public school system, like Stefania Raschilla, the DeBerry principal who has been brought in to turn things around. In the end, though, if you compare SICS and its successes to what has (or has not) happened at DeBerry over the past twenty years, I think it is fair to say that the school, the students, their parents, and their community would have been better served by embracing change and going with SABIS.

Finally, I want to say that I personally believe all of Springfield would be better off had not only the parents at DeBerry taken a risk on us, but had the entire district embraced a free market approach to public education where the best schools survive and replicate, while the worst ones go out of business. Yet this is not the trend at all.

CHAPTER 8

The stars in our halls

THROUGHOUT THIS BOOK, I have shared example after example of how union leaders and some local education officials and lawmakers fight charter school expansion, all while arguing that their position is in the best interest of the children. Using emotional, rather than rational arguments—that we care only for profits, not for children, for example—they try to prevent for-profit companies like ours from operating altogether and have been successful in some states.

What I have not yet said is that most of these people who so adamantly oppose us have never actually stepped inside one of our schools or met our students or their parents. They have not seen our brightly colored halls, our high-spirited, yet well-behaved students, or met our teachers and felt their enthusiasm and pride. We have invited them to come many times—indeed, we are always open for visitors—but sadly, hardly any of our critics take us up on this offer.

If they could see what we see when we walk through the halls of this Springfield school—the college acceptance letters on the walls or the teacher in the front hall telling anyone who will listen that his Model Congress team just won their sixth regional championship in a row and one of the students got $120,000 in scholarship money that very day—I think this would be a different debate. It would be a debate about how to improve quality at all charter and public schools so that more kids could go to college. Most of our opponents have never bothered to try to learn anything from our experiences. On the contrary, despite repeated attempts to share what we have learned over the years, the only thing Springfield's district schools have copied and credited us with is our school uniform policy. But there could be so much more.

And so in this chapter let me take you on a virtual tour of our Springfield school and introduce you to some of the people there. I wish you could see for yourselves the calm, orderly hum, the bright, clean halls, and feel the pride and enthusiasm of the people here, but at the very least I would like you to hear directly from our staff, students, and their parents. (And really, you are welcome to visit any time.)

The first thing you see when you walk into our Spring-field charter school is a big banner that says: "We Are College Bound." This is not random. We tell students from the moment they walk into this school that they are here to prepare for college, and we keep telling them every chance we get.

When 12th-graders are accepted to college, we ask them to volunteer to visit the lower grades to read their acceptance letters out loud and answer any questions younger students might have. Their acceptance letters are posted on a bulletin board in the hall. There is a "Senior Walk" just before graduation during which students fill the halls and the seniors walk the entire length of the building to a theme song of their choosing. The younger kids make signs to congratulate the seniors and give them high-fives as they pass by. You have to keep in mind that about half of these graduating seniors have been with us since kindergarten, and so it is as if they are walking back in time to get a pat on the back from a teacher who knew them when they were six years old. It is an extremely moving event.

Photo 8.1 SABIS International Charter School class of 2015 taking their "Senior Walk." Source: Courtesy of SABIS. Reproduced with permission.

Karen Reuter, the school's current director, recalls her first "Senior Walk," shortly after coming to SICS. "It's a beautiful thing," she says. "I was so overwhelmed. And I didn't know even one of those kids."

The school looks like something you would see in a wealthy

suburb. The pale brick, 180,000 square foot building sits on a 40-acre woodland property. SABIS built the school by taking an enormous risk by using its own assets to secure the loan. Today the charter school's board owns it.

The school has two gyms, two cafeterias, two large music rooms, and multiple science and computer labs. Many public schools have these facilities too, but what most urban schools lack is that calm sense of purpose that permeates our halls. It helps, I think, that we have high standards and a demanding curriculum. The kids cannot afford to mess around much or they will fall behind.

Gina Martin-Ryan is the student life coordinator, an administrator who encourages students to take part in improving their school environment and works with them to become responsible, model citizens. Coming from a district middle school, she says her first impression of the school was that it was quiet, even when kids were switching classes. She says she delivered her résumé in person to SICS and knew from the moment she walked into the building that she wanted to work there. "It's just a healthy environment. It was calm, peaceful, well cared for. People interacting, not ignoring each other. Kids staying after school because of a connection to their school community."

A frequent criticism of for-profit schools like ours is that we are not in it for the kids, but for the money, and that we will pocket any surpluses. Karen Reuter would assure you that this is not the case. "We run lean and mean here," she says, "but I've never felt the children weren't getting what they needed."

In 2014, Reuter got approval for her idea to use a $30,000 surplus to expand the school's music program, including buying a used Steinway piano. Reuter says the vendor was so happy the piano would be played and loved by students instead of becoming "an ornament in someone's home" that he knocked $3,000 off the price. What Reuter likes best, she says, is the freedom she has to effect change in ways she sees fit, not in ways dictated to her by union representatives. She says things were very different when she taught in New York City's public schools.

She talks about how in New York she used to tutor students from her class after school. Then, one day, a union official approached her and said she could not continue because it was not part of her union contract. Reuter thought that sounded ridiculous. She was not taking any money and it was her own time. But the union representative would not budge, so Reuter got the kids to meet her in secret at a coffee shop.

At SABIS, she says, "I'm not caught in a bureaucratic process so that I can't make a good idea come to life. That's what I value so much about being part of the charter school model."

Reuter has asked me to tell you this (following another legislative move to ban for-profits in Massachusetts):

I ask the lawmakers to come to my school and meet with these kids and tell me they think these kids should go back to the traditional public schools in Springfield and try to make it there. I'm sure there are kids who make it there, and even thrive. But it's despite the odds. There's not the same structure in place for them to thrive as they do here.

If you visited SICS, you might meet parents like Lorna Lewis, an immigrant from Jamaica. She first heard of SICS at a nail salon and learned that it was a college-preparatory school. She says she liked the sound of college prep, explaining: "At least I know where my children are going."

She put her daughter Ashley on the waiting list and two years later got a place. To be safe, she asked her daughter's old school, a private Catholic one, to hold open her child's place for six months. A priest agreed, saying: "I know you won't like it there." Lewis never looked back. Her daughter blossomed, she says, got As, and made friends. Today she is studying political science at Providence College and plans to be a lawyer.

Lewis says she likes the fact that the school challenges her children. Her son Antonio was a straight-A student at his old school but struggled in math when he first got to SICS. With help from the school, though, he eventually excelled in the subject and went on to earn a full scholarship to Bates College. Eventually, all four of Lewis's children would attend SICS. She calls that day in the nail salon "a blessing."

Then there is Ellen McDonald, chair of the SICS board of trustees, whose son attended the school. She and her husband had been planning to leave the city if their son did not get into SICS. They were even willing to downsize in order to live in a more expensive suburb with better public schools. They thought the elementary school options in the city were fine, but did not feel the same about the middle schools. Her husband is a bricklayer for the city, and while working in classrooms at local middle schools saw things that concerned him. Too often, misbehaving students monopolized teachers' attention, he felt, while students who seemed ahead of the lessons were ignored. "That was not the vision we had for our child," says McDonald.

Her son got a place at SICS in kindergarten and the family stayed in Springfield. Asked whether she had doubts about the school or the for-profit company running it, given so much negative press at the time, she answered: "I'm not an expert in

Photo 8.2 SABIS International Charter School graduates.

Source: Courtesy of SABIS. Reproduced with permission.

education, but I can at least discern what is real and what isn't real. And in my mind, if you have a union that is so against it, there's something they are feeling threatened by."

In 2015, her son Joseph started at the University of Massachusetts Lowell, where he is studying to be an engineer. Because he took Advanced Placement classes in high school, he started with enough credits to enter just short of being a first semester sophomore.

SICS, says McDonald, challenges kids to aspire to do more. "These kids are told from day one, 'You keep your cubby clean in kindergarten because you're going to need to keep your dorm room clean.' College! College! College! College! It gives them a future."

You are probably thinking by now that you would like to hear from the kids rather than the adults. So, here I would like you to meet a group of students who sat assembled one day, answering questions about how they felt about the school, its challenges and rewards, and shared their views on school choice.

The first thing that stands out about these kids, and indeed stands out about most of our students, is their confidence. Typically, teenagers are hard to draw out, but when you get our students together, it is difficult to give everyone a turn because they all have so much to say.

First, they will tell you that it is challenging at SICS. We do a lot of testing to be sure that our students are learning and to prepare them for statewide and college entrance exams. When Yaslin Alicea-Hidrovo, an 11th-grader, missed a week of school due to knee surgery, she says she missed lots of tests, including in physics and math. "I had to learn what I missed to be able to take those tests," she says, plus keeping on top of the current week, and so she spent a lot of time in after-school tutoring. She says that she eventually got back on track and, in her view, would rather try to rise to the occasion than fall to lesser expectations.

Nathan Johnson, another 11th-grader, who came to SICS in the eighth grade, says teachers at SICS have high expectations and believe that just passing is nowhere near good enough. "With my math teacher, if I get under an 80, she's like, 'What did I do wrong, Nathan? Tell me what I did wrong. What are you having trouble with?' When I went to Kennedy Middle School [a Springfield district school], if I got under an 80, or like a 60, they were like, 'Oh you passed, get out of here. If you passed, don't come to tutoring. You don't need any more help.'"

"This is a college-preparatory school," explains 10th-grader Christopher Gonzalez, who already knows that he wants to be a surgeon. "It's very obvious, and you'll know when you get here that you're not just here to get a diploma and do whatever after that. They really want you to succeed and go to college."

That is the other thing you soon notice. Our students are clear about where they are going, not just after high school, but after college. Their dreams are not small either, and they have ideas about how they are going to achieve them. Ask them about college and they rattle off a list of schools.

Senior Symone Green got early acceptance at Emerson College (though was still waiting to hear from Providence College and Brown at the time) and says she plans to be CEO of a nonprofit one day, as well as a mother. Savannah Taylor, an 11th-grader who has already visited Boston University, Fordham, and Wesleyan, among other schools, dreams of running her own corporation—or being on TV, possibly the next Beyoncé, she jokes—but "working for myself and contributing to my community." Chyanne Grant is only in the ninth grade but thinks that one day she might join the U.S. Air Force or some other arm of the military.

These kids are all minority students from low-income families, like so many students that fill the halls of Springfield's district public schools. Yet, they are beginning to feel a bit different from their old friends. Green says she feels that she has started to grow apart from her friends at other public, and even some area private schools, because she takes school so seriously and senses she is on a different path.

Taylor talks of a friend at a local public school, whom she describes as a good student who takes school seriously but cannot get her head around college. Taylor says she sat her friend down and asked her what she wanted to do after high school, and her friend said: "Well, I can't major in cheerleading." Says Taylor, who spends her spare time interning at a nearby Fortune 100 company: "She doesn't see any other benefits of college for her personally."

Johnson says many of his old friends at other schools dream of playing professional basketball or football, only to realize too late that they are not big enough or fast enough, and then do not have the grades and have not even looked at colleges. Johnson, who is captain of his football team, joined SICS in the ninth grade and recalls how straight away he had to go to a college fair. At the time, he says, he did not know a lot of the schools at the fair even existed. "The only colleges I knew were like the big football programs like FSU [Florida State University], Alabama, Mississippi State, stuff like that, that I see on TV," he says. Attending the school has changed his thinking. Today he says he wants to be a physician's assistant when he grows up and hopes to get into a university with a good medical program like Cornell.

Finally, what are these kids' views on school choice and whether charter schools should be allowed to expand more freely? Not surprisingly, they overwhelmingly support school choice, as they are benefitting from it.

Grant says she is a big supporter because she likes the challenges and feels she was coasting at her old public school. She says this, even though for her these challenges have at times seemed overwhelming and she has had to reach out for extra help from staff. "I like challenges; I actually do," she says, "and I wasn't getting the challenges that I needed for me to be where I am now."

Taylor says she thinks there should be a variety of options to suit all types of student "because some kids just cannot conform to a charter school's expectations and I feel like that's O.K." Green says that she is a "strong advocate of charter schools, obviously" and they get you ready for college, but says that vocational schools are a good option for students who want to be career-ready, but who are not academically strong.

Gonzalez believes lawmakers must offer parents a choice and says that if schools like SICS "were no longer in existence, then I feel that would be a great injustice." While Alicea-Hidrovo believes it is only right to give parents who cannot afford private schools something similar for their children. "It's even better than some private schools," she says.

But it is Nathan Johnson's argument that I would like to leave you with because of the simplicity and power of his words. He says:

> We live in a free country. I believe everyone should have a choice.

CHAPTER 9

Final thoughts and policy recommendations

W HY ARE PEOPLE SO AFRAID of a free market for public education when there is clearly so much to gain and so little to lose? I began this book by sharing some alarming statistics and would like to start this final chapter with a reminder of the magnitude of the problem:

- A quarter of American high school seniors lack basic reading skills, while 35 percent of them lack basic math skills.[1]

- American 15-year-olds rank below their peers from the world's top 20 most developed countries, performing below average in math and just about average in reading and science.[2]

- While graduation rates have never been better, with more than three million students receiving high school diplomas in 2014, one-third of the nation's eligible black and Hispanic young men failed to graduate.[3]

- In many states, one-third of students from low-income families fail to graduate.[4]

- Despite some progress, black 12th-graders are still roughly 2.5 times more likely than their white counterparts to perform below the basic level in math and reading.[5]

- Hispanic 12th-graders are about twice as likely to perform below the basic level in math and reading compared to their white counterparts.[6]

- The gap between minority and white students who earned a bachelor's or higher degree expanded significantly between 1990 and 2013.[7]

- Wealth inequality by race and ethnicity has grown since 2007, with white households currently holding 17 times the wealth of black households, the highest disparity since 1989.[8]

Failing to improve America's public schools and close achievement gaps has serious economic and social consequences. Just as I was finishing work on this book, the *New York Times* wrote that narrowing the achievement gap would add trillions of dollars to the U.S. economy.[9] Citing a new study, the article said that if America could match the student performance scores of Canada, as measured by the Organization for Economic Co-operation and Development (OECD), it would mean an additional 6.7 percent in gross domestic product (GDP)—a cumulative increase of $10 trillion (taking inflation into account) by 2050. Just moving up a few places on the OECD rankings, where the U.S. lags far behind Korea, Poland, and Slovenia, could add 1.7 percent to the nation's GDP over the next 35 years.[10]

But it is the social consequences that should cause the

greatest alarm. Public schools—historically viewed as the great democratizer in helping lift kids out of poverty—are not doing their jobs. Just consider this: In New York City, where leaders in 2014 trumpeted a four-year graduation rate of 68 percent, at least one-third of those graduates were not considered ready for college.[11, 12] Progress or not, these numbers should be mortifying to the leaders of one of the world's wealthiest cities.

It is not just New York City. There are more than a dozen other large cities with lower graduation rates.[13] Meanwhile, the achievement gap between high- and low-income students has widened by about 40 percent,[14] and already it seems there is one likely outcome: The emergence of the widest wealth gap between upper-income and lower-income families in thirty years.[15]

While there are many contributing factors to explain this growing gap, there is no prospect of reducing it without substantially improving the ability of the country's most disadvantaged citizens to earn and save, and this means dramatically improving education, including teaching higher and more relevant skills.

Public school officials, as well as many lawmakers, have brought a lot of these problems on themselves by failing to reform faster and by allowing teachers unions to dictate school policies and essentially block all education reform unless it directly benefits the teachers.

What is the answer? One obvious way to raise education standards is by mobilizing all available resources, including, and especially from, the private sector, to help build new public schools and rehabilitate existing failing ones via charter schools. I fully appreciate that not everyone sees that for-profit companies are the answer, but in fact, there is no rational objection to them.

For-profits already play a key role in every other area of public school life. The companies that produce the books and computers and run the cafeterias, for example, not to mention the taxpayer-funded pre-school and special education programs, make a profit. For-profit companies run hospitals and build roads and even explore space. What is the problem here? Is public education, even when it is failing so many students, somehow sacred?

There is nothing sacred about public schools that should prevent for-profits from helping raise education standards. On the contrary, for-profits bring discipline to a market and increase accountability. It is this discipline that keeps school operators sharp, and motivated to treat teachers well and ensure students are learning; otherwise, the operator would be out of business. Indeed, profit is the very thing that allows companies like SABIS to grow and thrive, be innovative, and guard against complacency. If your very existence depends on staying ahead of the competition, then you cannot be complacent. Ultimately, it is profit that will help to build new and better schools with higher standards.

The primary reason that for-profits are not more involved is because so many public school officials and union leaders— fearing competition that could lead to a loss of jobs, control over district budgets, and control over the school systems they manage—have fought tooth and nail to keep them out. More than that, they have advocated policies that undermine the entire charter school sector. These policies range from arbitrary caps on the number of students in a district who can attend charter schools to outright bans on for-profit education providers; as well as the exclusion of charter schools altogether in some districts and states. More often than not, resistance to a free market for public education has nothing to do with what is best for the kids. It is about adults protecting their own jobs, pay checks, and spheres of influence.

Leaders should talk less about putting kids first and actually put them first. Instead of bowing to special interest groups, they should create policies to build a level playing field and a competitive education environment so that over time the best schools—those that achieve results and do so consistently— will flourish and student achievement will rise.

With that final thought, I would like to propose some policy recommendations to strengthen the charter school sector and help it operate more effectively. I start with three big picture suggestions followed by more specific policy proposals. Their initial letters spell ACT SMART.

Please forgive this somewhat contrived acronym, but I feel a rallying cry is needed. More than twenty years ago a lot of smart people agreed that public education had stagnated and outsiders were required to make schools more competitive and innovative. Yet, here things stand, more than two decades into charter school reform, with not nearly enough to show for it.

The charter school movement, if permitted to fully flourish—meaning eliminating counterproductive restrictions and engaging all competitors, regardless of tax status—could go a long way to boosting academic achievement by all public school students. And so, enough with the smart talk, it is time to do something. It is time to ACT SMART.

Big Picture Recommendations

Accept that public schools need help

It is time to dramatically step up standards for all students, and particularly for poor and minority children in urban centers, if America is to thrive economically, socially, and culturally well into the next century.

Opponents will say that the education crisis has been exaggerated and that over time schools have improved, with more kids graduating now than ever before. It is true that more kids are graduating and that some are benefitting from good public education—particularly those children fortunate enough to live in America's more affluent suburbs—but it is not the kids in Greenwich, Connecticut, that should concern us. It is the ones in New Haven, where about one in four of the city's residents lives below the poverty line[16] and the district's dropout rate is about one in five, or 20 percent,[17] compared to a national average of about 7 percent.[18] It is also kids in America's wealthiest cities like New York and Los Angeles who are not graduating or who are graduating but without the skills to go to college. Public education is failing them and to pretend otherwise is wrong. These children deserve better.

Commit to the kids, not the adults

Politicians love to say it is all about the kids, but then support measures that undermine the development of what could be a robust and vibrant public education sector. Such moves serve only the interests of adults—or, more specifically, serve the interests of their most vocal and persuasive constituents, including union leaders, teachers, and school district officials.

These measures include capping the number of students that charter schools can educate in a district, including in districts with long waiting lists; granting far less funding for charter school students than for regular public school students; offering no facilities, much less tax exemptions for affordable loans to buy facilities; and permitting opaque authorizing procedures that too often let officials play favorites rather than award charters on merit. The end result is a hodgepodge of often counterproductive policies that vary by state and serve only to maintain the status quo. All politicians must rise above the fray when it comes to education. This problem is too big and too serious to keep playing politics. A bipartisan approach is essential if lawmakers are serious about better educating children.

Turn to the free market

Government officials have failed for too long to fix America's public education problem. The public sector has experimented with different testing methods and thrown increasing amounts of money at the problem but without significant results. Nonprofit charter school operators have done what they can, but their dependence on charitable contributions means that they do not scale easily. Despite a handful of exceptions, the result has been a fragmented market made up of mom-and-pop charter schools of varying quality. The problems facing public education today are too big and too complicated to be handled by government and nonprofits alone. The elephant in the room is the for-profit sector. Fear of for-profits in public education is unfounded and counterproductive. These companies are vital to turning around public education. Given a level playing field with fair rules and regulations, good education providers could compete to build mature companies offering education of a uniformly high quality. Finally, let me be clear: I am not suggesting eliminating public schools or ignoring the contribution of nonprofits. I am simply saying that America must turn to for-profits, just as the nation has done with every other sector.

Specific Policy Recommendations

Shift government's role to oversight only

Traditional public schools and charter schools should be held accountable for meeting high academic standards. It is government's role to set those standards, as well as to fairly and objectively monitor results, and to enforce accountability of all public schools.

It should not be government's role to tell organizations how to operate. Education providers should be free to run their schools however they see fit—hiring whomever they please or teaching classes using innovative methods—with government there to ensure schools show results. Government should not force school operators to adopt a governance structure that permits others to dictate how these results should be achieved.

Along these lines, authorizers should:

- Award charters directly to education providers that have the know-how to run schools and also have all the financial risk.

- If boards of trustees are required, their role should

be restricted to oversight, as in other industries. They should not have executive authority. There should be limited terms for board members, training, independent evaluations, and possibly accreditation.

Make charter schools and the entire sector more competitive

Government should remove barriers to entry for charter schools and change other restrictive operational requirements in order to attract more resources to the sector and help the best companies (for-profit or not) survive and flourish.

Here are some ways to do that:

- Shorten and streamline charter applications and approvals. For operators with proven track records of success, add a fast-track approval process with performance measurements based on fair, objective, and transparent metrics. Simplify the process by not permitting authorizers to create unnecessary work for education providers by demanding information already on file.

- Set the minimum charter term at ten years instead of the prevailing five years, which scares off investors and undermines sustainability.

- Seek solutions from companies that can best provide them by not restricting charters to nonprofit operators, as some state lawmakers have done and other state lawmakers are considering, thereby stifling innovation and undermining scalability and sustainability.

Attract capital

The biggest barrier to building and expanding charter schools is a lack of real estate and real estate funding. Some district officials let abandoned school buildings sit vacant rather than make them available to charter schools, even though inner city neighborhoods would clearly be better off with more schools and fewer vacant buildings. Too few states allow charter schools to borrow money at government rates to build facilities. The outcome sometimes is that charter school operators with already approved charters cannot open schools because they cannot find or afford facilities.

Government should create tax incentives to attract donors to help finance facilities for approved charter schools.

- Tax incentives would encourage donors to put money into a special real estate fund that for-profit and nonprofit companies could access.

- It would be attractive to donors who prefer funding concrete things like buildings rather than ongoing expenses.

- Donors would be helping to improve student welfare, as well as revitalizing cities and employing workers.

Remove restrictions that limit growth

The market (parents) should decide how many charter schools a district needs, not bureaucrats or lobbyists representing special interest groups (e.g., unions). As it stands, more than 600,000 kids are on waiting lists for charter schools across

America.[19] A family that wants their child to attend a higher-performing charter school can only sit and hope fate intervenes and their child's name is one of the lucky few picked in a lottery.

- Caps that restrict the number of students admitted to charter schools should be removed.

- Caps on the number of students and charter schools in a district should also be removed, along with the often arbitrary formulas that limit schools to particular neighborhoods.

Treat all public schools equally

For long-term success and sustainability, charter schools, whether for-profit or nonprofit, should be treated like traditional public schools when it comes to funding, facilities, transportation, and taxation, as indeed they are all public schools.

- 100 percent of per pupil funding should follow the student. Charter schools are public schools and their students should not be penalized financially for attending them.

- Student funding should be paid to education providers in advance, not in arrears, as is the practice in some states.

- Per pupil funding should be fixed from the beginning of the school year and should not change. This happens frequently when states cut per pupil funding mid-year. This makes it operationally challenging for companies trying to meet payrolls and run schools.

- Charter schools, regardless of their tax status, should

be taxed like traditional public schools when it comes to property tax, income tax, sales tax, etc.

■ Transportation should be available to charter school students who live within a district.

■ Public school facilities no longer in use by local districts should be available to charter schools. These buildings were built and funded by taxpayers, and all children—no matter what type of public school they choose—should benefit from them.

Conclusion

So, why are people so opposed to a free market for public education?

Perhaps it is simply a question of time. Controversy often accompanies competitive for-profit companies entering traditional monopolies or public sectors. But these concerns subside. Today, few people think twice about who is making a profit when calling a friend, riding a subway, driving on a highway, or seeing a doctor. Change provokes fear, sometimes irrational fear. With time, though, most people see that services to the public should be efficient and that efficiency is best served through competition.

Certainly, enough time has passed for charter schools. One in 20 kids in America attends a charter school. Charter schools are already a critical part of the U.S. public education system. Faced with chronic achievement gaps that undermine this country, time is better spent improving rather than opposing them. Oversight of all schools is necessary and should constantly be improved. The focus, however, should be on creating a thriving free market—one that embraces all types of providers, and one that rewards winners, eliminates losers, and ultimately lifts kids out of poverty rather than traps them in it forever.

I find it especially strange to have this debate in America. America, after all, was built on free enterprise. America leapt ahead because it embraced the free market when other countries imposed state monopolies—in telecommunications, railroads, electrical power generation and transmission, gas distribution, oil, coal, and steel industries. America has always understood the benefits of the free market. Why does it forget those lessons now when the stakes are so high? Nobel Prize winning economist Milton Friedman succinctly reminds us:

> *So that the record of history is absolutely crystal clear. That there is no alternative way, so far discovered, of improving the lot of the ordinary people that can hold a candle to the productive activities that are unleashed by a free enterprise system.*

Notes

Introduction

1. Violent crime in Springfield, Massachusetts peaked in 1997, but has since declined dramatically. Retrieved from www.masslive.com/news/index.ssf/2013/09/fbi_data_springfield_saw_near.html

2. The full legal name of the company is SABIS® Educational Systems, Inc. All references to "our" schools refer to a school that is part of the SABIS® Network in the U.S. SABIS is an amalgamation of the names of the two families that established the company: Saad and Bistany.

3. Rich, Motoko (January 16, 2015). Percentage of Poor Students in Public Schools Rises, *The New York Times*.

4. O'Day, Brendan F. (1997). *Bringing a Charter School Home: Politics and Finances in Springfield,* Harvard Graduate School of Education, Cambridge, MA.

5. *U.S. News & World Report* awarded the SABIS® International Charter School a silver medal in its "Best High Schools" report from 2010 to 2015.

6. Massachusetts Department of Elementary and Secondary Education. Retrieved from profiles.doe.mass.

edu/analysis/default.aspx?orgcode=02810045&orgtype code=6&

7. Level 4 schools are Massachusetts's worst-performing schools, based on an analysis of four-year trends in absolute achievement, student growth, and improvement trends, as measured by the Massachusetts Comprehensive Assessment System (MCAS). A Level 4 school may be reclassified as Level 5 by the Commissioner on behalf of the state Board of Elementary and Secondary Education if it fails to improve or if district conditions make it unlikely that the school will make significant improvement without a Level 5 designation.

8. Education Expenditures by Country, National Center for Education Statistics (January 2014). Retrieved from nces.ed.gov/programs/coe/indicator_cmd.asp

9. SABIS employs different operating models in the private and public sectors in different countries. While the U.S. charter model dictates that profits remain on the board's accounts, other models do not include this stipulation. In such cases, SABIS is free to determine how profits can be used in the best interest of students and the business.

10. Audits are independent, available to the public, and submitted to authorizers. The annual audit is a summary of the school's financial results, and the CPA reviews the results in detail (i.e., accounts for "every dime"). Public charter schools are held to the same governmental auditing standards as traditional public schools. These audit guidelines are established by the Governmental Accounting Standards Board (GASB).

Chapter 1

1. National Commission on Excellence in Education (1983). *A Nation at Risk: The Imperative for Educational Reform*, U.S. Department of Education, Washington, D.C.

2. Gantert, Tom (October 8, 2014). Union Leader Celebrates Failing School's Performance, *Michigan Capitol Confidential*.

3. *The Nation's Report Card: 2013 Mathematics and Reading: Grade 12 Assessment* (May 2014). The National Center for Education Statistics, U.S. Department of Education. Retrieved from www.nationsreportcard.gov/reading_math_g12_2013/#

4. Math performance in 2013 cannot be compared with 1992 because changes were made to the math framework in 2005.

5. *The Nation's Report Card: 2013 Mathematics and Reading: Grade 12 Assessment*, op. cit.

6. Ibid.

7. Ibid.

8. Functional illiteracy is defined by Diane McGuinness (2004), *Early Reading Instruction*, MIT Press, Cambridge, MA, and others, as performing "below Basic" on the National Assessment of Education Progress (NAEP) reading test.

9. *The Nation's Report Card: 2013 Mathematics and Reading: Grade 12 Assessment*, op. cit.

10. *Statement from the Education Trust on 12th Grade Reading and Mathematics Results From the 2013 National*

Assessment of Educational Progress (October 2014). The Education Trust.

11. Ibid.

12. *The Nation's Report Card: 2013 Mathematics and Reading: Grade 12 Assessment*, op. cit.

13. Ibid.

14. Kena, Grace, et al. (May 2014). *The Condition of Education 2014* (NCES 2014–083), U.S. Department of Education, National Center for Education Statistics. Washington, D.C.

15. Ibid., p. 2.

16. Montenegro, Claudio E., and Patrinos, Harry A. (September 2014). *Comparable Estimates of Returns to Schooling around the World*, World Bank Policy Research Working Paper No. 7020.

17. Fry, Richard, and Kochhar, Rakesh (December 2014). *Wealth Inequality Has Widened along Racial, Ethnic Lines since End of Great Recession*, Pew Research Center.

18. Stetser, M., and Stillwell, R. (2014). *Public High School Four-Year On-Time Graduation Rates and Event Dropout Rates: School Years 2010–11 and 2011–12*. First Look (NCES 2014–391). U.S. Department of Education. Washington, D.C: National Center for Education Statistics.

19. Fry and Kochhar, *Wealth Inequality Has Widened along Racial, Ethnic Lines since End of Great Recession*, op. cit.

20. Stetser and Stillwell, *Public High School Four-Year On-Time Graduation Rates and Event Dropout Rates: School Years 2010–11 and 2011–12*, op. cit., p. 4.

21. Ibid.

22. Layton, Lyndsey (April 28, 2014). National High School Graduation Rates at Historic High, But Disparities Still Exist, *The Washington Post.*

23. Balfanz, Robert (June 7, 2014). Stop Holding Us Back, *The New York Times.*

24. Ibid.

25. Danziger, Sheldon, and Wimer, Christopher (2014). Poverty, pp. 13–18 in *The Poverty and Inequality Report: A Special Issue of Pathways Magazine.* Vol. 1, *State of the Union,* edited by Varner, Charles; Mattingly, Marybeth; and Grusky, David. Stanford, CA: Stanford Center on Poverty and Inequality.

26. *NAEP as an Indicator of Students' Academic Preparedness for College* (2014). National Assessment Governing Board, National Center for Education Statistics, U.S. Department of Education.

27. Sparks, D., and Malkus, N. (2013). Statistics in Brief: First-Year Undergraduate Coursetaking: 1999–2000, 2003–04, 2007–08 (NCES 2013–013), U.S. Department of Education, National Center for Education Statistics.

28. Balfanz, Robert, et al. (2015). *Building a Grad Nation: Progress and Challenge in Ending the High School Dropout Epidemic—2015 Annual Update.* Washington, D.C.: Civic Enterprises, the Everyone Graduates Center at Johns Hopkins University School of Education, America's Promise Alliance, and the Alliance for Excellent Education.

29. *NAEP as an Indicator of Students' Academic Preparedness for College,* op. cit.

30. Paulson, Amanda (May 14, 2014). Less than 40 percent of 12th-graders Ready for College, Analysis Finds, *The Christian Science Monitor*.

31. Schleicher, Andreas, et al. (December 2013). *OECD PISA 2012 Results*, OECD Publishing, Organization for Cooperation and Development (OECD).

32. Ibid.

33. Ibid.

34. Chappell, Bill (December 3, 2013). U.S. Students Slide in Global Ranking on Math, Reading, Science, *NPR*.

35. Ibid.

36. Ibid.

37. *The Threat of Educational Stagnation and Complacency*, Remarks of U.S. Secretary of Education Arne Duncan at the release of the 2012 Program for International Student Assessment (PISA) (December 3, 2013). U.S. Department of Education.

38. Chappell, U.S. Students Slide in Global Ranking on Math, Reading, Science, op. cit.

39. National Science Board (February 2014). *Science and Engineering Indicators 2014*, National Science Foundation (NSB 14–01).

40. Ibid.

41. Friedman, Thomas L. (June 27, 2009). Invent, Invent, Invent, *The New York Times*.

42. Ruiz, Neil G. (August 2014). *The Geography of Foreign Students in U.S. Higher Education: Origins and Destinations*, The Brookings Institution.

43. McGrady, Clyde (September 25, 2014). Without H-1B Visa Changes Microsoft May Continue Foreign Expansion, *Roll Call.*

44. Reardon, Sean F. (2014). Education, pp. 51–6, in *The Poverty and Inequality Report: A Special Issue of Pathways Magazine.* Vol. 1, *State of the Union*, edited by Varner, Charles; Mattingly, Marybeth; and Grusky, David. Stanford, CA: Stanford Center on Poverty and Inequality.

45. Suitts, Steve (2015). *A New Majority Research Bulletin: Low Income Students Now a Majority in the Nation's Public Schools.* Southern Education Foundation.

46. The Southern Education Foundation reported that 51 percent of students in pre-kindergarten through 12th grade in the 2012–13 school year were from low-income homes, defined as being eligible for a federal program that provides free or subsidized lunches.

47. Varner, Mattingly, and Grusky. Executive Summary, pp. 3–7 in *The Poverty and Inequality Report: A Special Issue of Pathways Magazine.*

48. A Stanford Center on Poverty and Inequality "State of the Union" report was released in 2015. It focused on making state-by-state comparisons, and did not suggest significant changes from the 2014 report.

49. Varner, Mattingly, and Grusky, *The Poverty and Inequality Report*, op. cit., p. 6.

50. Reardon, Education, op. cit., p. 56.

51. National Commission on Excellence in Education, *A Nation at Risk: The Imperative for Educational Reform*, op. cit.

52. Coulson, Andrew J. (March 2014). *State Education Trends, Academic Performance and Spending Trends over the Past 40 Years*, Cato Institute, Policy Analysis No. 746, Cato Institute.

53. *Federal, State, and Local K-12 School Finance Overview* (April 2014). Federal Education Budget Project, New America Foundation.

54. Ibid.

55. Chappell, U.S. Students Slide in Global Ranking on Math, Reading, Science, op. cit.

56. Coulson, *State Education Trends, Academic Performance and Spending Trends over the Past 40 Years*, op. cit.

57. Zuckerberg stipulated that he would release the money as matching funds against additional dollars raised.

58. Russakoff, Dale (May 19, 2014). Schooled, *The New Yorker*.

59. Gates Foundation (May 29, 2009). Teachers Trump Class Size. *eSchool News*.

60. Mark Zuckerberg Announces $100 Million Grant (September 24, 2010). *The Oprah Winfrey Show*.

61. Donor list, Teach for America, 2012/2013. Retrieved from www.teachforamerica.org/support-us/donors

62. Winerip, Michael (July 11, 2010). A Chosen Few Are Teaching for America, *The New York Times*.

63. Motoko, Rich (February 5, 2015). Fewer Top Graduates Want to Join Teach for America, *The New York Times*.

64. Ibid.

65. Strauss, Valerie (January 7, 2012). A Decade of No Child Left Behind: Lessons from a Policy Failure, *The Washington Post*.

66. Boehner, John (April 2004). *Frequently Asked Questions about No Child Left Behind*, U.S. House Committee on Education & the Workforce.

67. Kamenetz, Anya (October 11, 2014). It's 2014. All Children Are Supposed To Be Proficient. What Happened? *NPR*.

68. *No Child Left Behind Overview* (April 2014). Federal Education Budget Project, New America Foundation.

69. *No Child Left Behind Funding* (April 2014). Federal Education Budget Project, New America Foundation.

70. Hanushek, Eric A. (June 30, 2014). How Teachers Unions Use "Common Core" to Undermine Reform, *The Wall Street Journal*.

71. Quijano, Elaine (March 2, 2015). Leery Parents Join Nationwide Boycott of Common Core Exam, *CBS News*.

72. Riley, Jason (February 17, 2015). Common Core Has a Central Problem, *The Wall Street Journal*.

73. Cremata, Edward, et al. (June 2013). *National Charter School Study 2013*, Center for Research on Education Outcomes, CREDO at Stanford University. Stanford University, Stanford, CA.

74. Ozimek, Adam (January 11, 2015). The Unappreciated Success of Charter Schools, *Forbes*.

75. Hudson, Jerome (October 3, 2014). Thousands of Charter School Supporters Protest Mayor de Blasio in New York City, *Daily Surge*.

76. The figure of 143,000 students attending failing public schools is based on the statewide English and math exams and college-readiness statistics and was calculated by the nonprofit advocacy group Families for Excellent Schools. In June 2015, that number was updated to 148,000 students attending 390 severely failing public schools in New York City.

77. Hudson, Thousands of Charter School Supporters Protest Mayor de Blasio in New York City, op. cit.

78. Ibid.

79. National Commission on Excellence in Education, *A Nation at Risk*, op. cit.

80. *The Nation's Report Card: 2013 Mathematics and Reading: Grade 12 Assessment*, op. cit.

Chapter 2

1. Hussar, William J., and Bailey, Tabitha M. (February 2014). *Projections of Education Statistics to 2022* (NCES 2014–051). U.S. Department of Education, National Center for Education Statistics. Washington, D.C., U.S. Government Printing Office.

2. Record Number of Homeless Students Reported in Nevada Schools, (October 8, 2014). *Elko Daily Free Press*.

3. Bassuk, Ellen L., DeCandia, Carmela J., Beach, Corey A., and Berman, Fred (November 2014). *America's Youngest Outcasts, A Report Card on Child Homelessness*, American Institutes for Research, The National Center on Family Homelessness.

4. Hussar and Bailey, *Projections of Education Statistics to 2022*, op. cit., p. 38.

5. *Children Living in Poverty* (last updated May 2014). U.S. Department of Education, National Center for Education Statistics. Washington, D.C. Retrieved from nces.ed.gov/ programs/coe/indicator_cce.asp

6. Hussar and Bailey, *Projections of Education Statistics to 2022*, op. cit., p. 5.

7. Ibid.

8. Ibid., p. 6.

9. Kena, G., Aud, S., Johnson, F., Wang, X., Zhang, J., Rathbun, A., Wilkinson-Flicker, S., and Kristapovich, P. (May 2014). *The Condition of Education 2014* (NCES 2014–083). U.S. Department of Education, National Center for Education Statistics. Washington, D.C.

10. Suitts, *A New Majority Research Bulletin: Low Income Students Now a Majority in the Nation's Public Schools*, op. cit.

11. This figure refers to the total unduplicated, statewide number of homeless students who were enrolled in public schools in local education agencies (LEAs). McKinney–Vento grants support state efforts to provide equal access to free and appropriate public education to homeless students and to gather information about those students and their needs. See eddataexpress.ed.gov/data-element-explorer.cfm/tab/data/deid/4569

12. Reardon, Sean F. (May 2013). The Widening Income Achievement Gap, *Faces of Poverty*, Vol. 70, No. 8.

13. Crouch, Ron, Banks Zakariya, Sally, and Jiandani, Joyti (updated May 2012). *The United States of Education: The Changing Demographics of the United States and Their Schools*, Center for Public Education.

14. Michigan Association of Public School Academies, Lansing, MI. Retrieved from www.charterschools.org/school-services/faq/1-general/4-how-many-charter-schools-are-there-in-michigan

15. Neher, Jack (March 2015). State Superintendent Calls for Moratorium on New Charter Schools, *Michigan Radio*.

16. National Alliance for Public Charter Schools, Washington, D.C. Retrieved from www.publiccharters.org/get-the-facts/public-charter-schools/faqs

17. Miron, G., and Gulosino, C. (November 2013). *Profiles of For-Profit and Nonprofit Education Management Organizations: Fourteenth Edition—2011–2012*. Boulder, CO: National Education Policy Center.

18. National Alliance for Public Charter Schools, op. cit.

19. Laday, Jason (March 9, 2014). Camden Superintendent: A "Dramatic Lack of Rigor" in District Schools, *South Jersey Times*.

20. Ibid.

21. *FAQS*, National Alliance for Public Charter Schools. Retrieved from www.publiccharters.org/get-the-facts/public-charter-schools/faqs

22. Ibid.

23. Ibid.

24. *Separating Fact & Fiction: What You Need to Know about Charter Schools* (2014). National Alliance for Public Charter Schools, Washington, D.C.

25. *Pre-K Funding from State and Federal Sources* (April 2014). Federal Education Budget Project, New America Foundation.

26. Hess, Frederick M., and Horn, Michael B. (2013). *Private Enterprise and Public Education*, Teachers College Press, Teachers College, Columbia University.

27. Shah, Nirvi (May 24, 2011). Districts Hire Outsider to Trim Special Ed. Costs, *Education Week*.

28. According to the U.S. Department of Education, to be deemed highly qualified under the No Child Left Behind provision, teachers must have: a bachelor's degree, full state certification or licensure, and prove that they know each subject they teach. NCLB defers to state law regarding certification.

29. Education Commission of the States (ECS) State Policy Database. Retrieved from www.ecs.org/ecs/ecscat.nsf/ WebTopicView?OpenView&count=-1&RestrictToCategor y=Teaching+Quality--Tenure+or+Continuing+Contract

30. *A Nation Accountable: Twenty-five Years after a Nation at Risk* (2008). U.S. Dept. of Education, Washington, D.C.

31. Ibid., p. 6.

32. Ibid.

33. Sweetland Edwards, Haley (October 30, 2014). The War on Teacher Tenure, *Time*.

34. A School Reform Landmark (June 10, 2014), Review & Outlook, *The Wall Street Journal*.

35. Ibid.

36. Ibid.

37. Ibid.

38. Court decision in *Vergara v. California* (June 2014), *The Washington Post*. Retrieved from apps.washingtonpost.com/g/documents/local/court-decision-in-vergara-v-california/1031

39. Batdorff, Meagan, et al. (April 2014). *Charter School Funding: Inequality Expands*, School Choice Demonstration Project, Department of Education Reform, University of Arkansas, Fayetteville, AR.

40. Hiltzik, Michael (October 22, 2013). The L.A. Schools' iPad Misadventure Is Looking a Lot More Expensive, *Los Angeles Times*.

41. Finley, Allysia (September 4, 2010). Broke—and Building the Most Expensive School in U.S. History, *The Wall Street Journal*.

42. Farmer, Blake (October 29, 2014). Andre Agassi's Pivot to Education Capitalist, *Marketplace*.

43. Garrison, Joey (September 17, 2014). Andre Agassi Embraces Investor-Led Approach to Schools, *The Tennessean, USA Today*.

44. Smith, Adam (1976 [first published 1776]). *An Inquiry into the Nature and Causes of the Wealth of Nations*, ed. Campbell, R. H. and Skinner, A. S., 2 vols, Glasgow Education of the Works and Correspondence of Adam Smith, Oxford University Press, Book 1, Chapter II, p. 19.

Chapter 3

1. Obama, Barack, Presidential Proclamation—National Charter Schools Week (May 7, 2012). The White House, Office of the Press Secretary.

2. Kerwin, Kara (May 4, 2015). Charter Schools Must Play a Bigger Role in U.S. Education, Special to *The Telegraph*.

3. Cremata et al., *National Charter School Study 2013*, op. cit.

4. As of April 2015, Kentucky, Montana, Nebraska, North Dakota, South Dakota, Vermont, and West Virginia had not enacted laws permitting charter schools to operate.

5. Ziebarth, Todd (January 2015). *Measuring up to the Model: A Ranking of State Charter School Laws*, National Alliance for Public Charter Schools, Washington, D.C.

6. Ibid.

7. Survey by the National Alliance for Public Charter Schools (June 2012). Washington, D.C. Retrieved from www.publiccharters.org/press/national-waitlist-figures-public-charter-schools-surpass-600000-students

8. Ziebarth, *Measuring up to the Model*, op. cit.

9. Massachusetts Charter Public School Association, Boston, MA.

10. Levenson, Michael (March 8, 2015). Civil Rights Fight Looms on Charter Schools Cap, *The Boston Globe*.

11. Illinois Network of Charter Schools, Chicago, IL. Retrieved from www.incschools.org/tableau/?post=32&type=policy_facts&index=0–0

12. Ibid.

13. The No Child Left Behind provision that teachers be "highly qualified," which requires a bachelor's degree, proven knowledge of the subjects taught, and full state certification or licensure for all teachers, defers to state charter law concerning certification requirements for charter school teachers. According to the National Alliance for Public Charter Schools, if a state does not require any charter teachers to be certified, NCLB docs not impose the certification mandate.

14. Goldhaber, D., Krieg, J., Theobald, R., and Brown, N. (2014). *The STEM and Special Education Teacher Pipelines: Why Don't We See Better Alignment Between Supply and Demand?* CEDR Working Paper 2014–3. University of Washington, Seattle, WA.

15. *Estimated Number of Public Charter Schools & Students 2014–2015*, Dashboard (February 2015). National Alliance for Public Charter Schools, Washington, D.C. Retrieved from www.publiccharters.org/wp-content/uploads/2015/02/open_closed_FINAL1.pdf

16. Brody, Leslie (November 11, 2014). Charter School Backed by the Teachers Union Is Still Struggling, *The Wall Street Journal*.

17. Ibid.

18. Saeidi, Mahsa (February 28, 2015). Controversial UFT Charter School in Brooklyn to Close Elementary and Middle Grades, *Time Warner Cable News, NY1*.

19. Batdorff et al., Charter School Funding, op. cit., p. 7.

20. Ibid.

21. Ibid.

22. Hollander, Sophia (September 15, 2014). Lawsuit Targets Funding Gap for Charter Schools, *The Wall Street Journal.*

23. Ibid.

24. Ibid.

25. Ziebarth, *Measuring up to the Model*, op. cit.

26. Hollander, Lawsuit Targets Funding Gap for Charter Schools, op. cit.

27. Neff, Blake (July 31, 2014). DC Charter Schools Sue City over Funding Gap, *The Daily Caller.*

28. Ibid.

29. Ibid.

30. Ibid.

31. Ibid.

32. *A Growing Movement: America's Largest Charter School Communities* (December 2014). National Alliance for Public Charter Schools, Washington, D.C.

33. *Estimated Number of Public Charter Schools & Students 2014–2015*, op. cit.

34. Ibid.

35. Ziebarth, *Measuring up to the Model*, op. cit.

36. Abraham, Reena, et al. (September 2014). *2014 Charter School Facility Finance Landscape, Educational Facilities Financing Center*, The Educational Facilities Financing Center of Local Initiatives Support Corporation.

37. Ibid., p. 1.

38. Moore, Harvin C. (September 13, 2010). A $585 Million Monument to Dysfunction—LA Opens its Newest School, *The Tranformation Times.*

39. Ziebarth, *Measuring up to the Model,* op. cit.

40. Transparent Charter Application Review, and Decisionmaking Processes, Measuring Up, National Alliance for Public Charter Schools, Washington, D.C. Retrieved from www.publiccharters.org/law-database/transparent-charter-application-review-decision-making-processes

41. Ibid.

42. Ibid.

43. Dodd, D. Aileen (June 3, 2011). Imperiled Charter Schools Told to Seek Local Approval, *The Atlanta-Journal Constitution.*

44. Valerio-Nowc, Lisa (October 27, 2014). Opinion: Who Loses with a Charter School Moratorium in Michigan, *Watchdog Wire Michigan.*

45. *Estimated Number of Public Charter Schools & Students, 2013–2014* (February 2014). National Alliance for Public Charter Schools, Dashboard, Washington, D.C. Retrieved from www.publiccharters.org/wp-content/uploads/2014/02/New-and-Closed-Report-February-20141.pdf

46. Ibid.

47. Harmon, Lawrence (October 18, 2014). Roadblock for Charter Schools, *The Boston Globe.*

48. Condi Rice: Today's True Racists Are Liberals Who Defend Teachers Unions (November 10, 2014), *Fox News*

Radio's "Kilmeade & Friends" via *Breitbart TV*, Breitbart News Network.

Chapter 4

1. Cremata et al., *National Charter School Study 2013*, op. cit.

2. Ibid.

3. Ibid., p. 16.

4. Ozimek. The Unappreciated Success of Charter Schools, op. cit.

5. Silvernail, David L., and Johnson, Amy F. (2014). *The Impacts of Public Charter Schools on Students and Traditional Public Schools: What Does the Empirical Evidence Tell Us?*, Maine Education Policy Research Institute in the Center for Education Policy, Applied Research, and Evaluation (CEPARE) in the School of Education and Human Development, University of Southern Maine.

6. Ibid., p. 17.

7. Ozimek, The Unappreciated Success of Charter Schools, op. cit.

8. Cremata et al., *National Charter School Study 2013*, op. cit.

9. For the full methodology, see http://credo.stanford.edu/documents/NCSS%202013%20Final%20Draft.pdf

10. Cremata et al., *National Charter School Study 2013*, op. cit.

11. Stetser and Stillwell, *Public High School Four-Year On-Time Graduation Rates and Event Dropout Rates: School Years 2010–11 and 2011–12*, p. 4.

12. Cremata et al., *National Charter School Study 2013*, op. cit.

13. The 2009 report covered 16 states, while a new examination in the 2013 report covered 27 states.

14. Angrist, Joshua D., et al. (May 2013). *Charter Schools and the Road to College Readiness: The Effects on College Preparation, Attendance and Choice*, MIT's School Effectiveness and Inequality Initiative (SEII). The Boston Foundation.

15. Ibid.

16. Ibid.

17. Hoxby, Caroline M., Murarka, Sonali, and Kang, Jenny (September 2009). *How New York City's Charter Schools Affect Achievement, August 2009 Report*, Second report in series. Cambridge, MA: New York City Charter Schools Evaluation Project.

18. The report's authors created something called the Scarsdale–Harlem Achievement gap, which refers to the approximate 35-point achievement gap between students in one of New York City's most affluent suburbs, Scarsdale, and students in Harlem, where many of the city's charter schools are located. If charter schools in New York City improved students' scores by 30 points, then their students will have made up about 86 percent of the Scarsdale–Harlem achievement gap. The test score gap between Scarsdale and Harlem varies from grade

to grade and year to year, so the 35-point gap is only approximate. Scarsdale was used not to analyze that district's achievement, but simply as a mnemonic device, according to the report's authors.

19. Kingsland, Neerav (2015). The New Orleans Case for All-Charter School Districts, *Education Next*, Summer, Vol. 15, No. 3.

20. Ibid.

21. Ibid.

22. Ibid.

23. Ibid.

24. Ibid.

25. Cremata et al., *National Charter School Study 2013*, op. cit., p. 52.

26. Ziebarth, *Measuring up to the Model*, op. cit.

27. Cremata et al., *National Charter School Study 2013*, op. cit., p. 52.

28. Ibid.

29. Ziebarth, *Measuring up to the Model*, op. cit.

30. Cremata et al., *National Charter School Study 2013*, op. cit., p. 52.

Chapter 5

1. Stergios, Jim (March 3, 2013). *Why Do District Superintendents Oppose Charter Schools?* Pioneer Institute.

2. Nembirkow did not deny the charter application, as charters are approved or rejected by the Massachusetts Board of Elementary and Secondary Education.

However, as the Brockton School Superintendent, Nembirkow marshaled opposition that likely led to the denial of the charter.

3. Staff (February 16, 2012). Proving themselves by performing, *The Boston Globe*.

4. Winkler, Amber M., Scull, Janie, and Zeehandelaar, Dara (October 2012), *How Strong Are U.S. Teachers Unions? A State-By-State Comparison*, Thomas Fordham Institute.

5. National Education Association homepage, www.nea.org/home/1594.htm

6. Center for Responsive Politics' Open Secrets.org database. Retrieved from www.opensecrets.org/orgs/list.php

7. The American Federation of Teachers homepage, www.aft.org/about

8. Center for Responsive Politics, op. cit.

9. *Heavy-Hitters: Top All Time Donors, 1989–2014*, Center for Responsive Politics. Based on data released by the Federal Election Commission on February 2, 2015. Retrieved from www.opensecrets.org/orgs/list.php

10. Ibid.

11. Nankin, Jesse, and Kjellman Schmidt, Krista (April 2009), History of U.S. Gov't Bailouts, *ProPublica*.

12. *Heavy-Hitters: Top All Time Donors, 1989–2014*, op. cit.

13. Mooney, Brian C. (November 1, 2006). 2 Unions Spending Big for Patrick, *The Boston Globe*.

14. Bernstein, David S. (December 13, 2006). Deval's Dance with Labor, *The Phoenix*.

15. Chieppo, Charles and Gass, Jamie (October 11, 2013). Guest Opinion: Patrick's Dismantling of Education Reform Has Consequences, *The Herald News*.

16. Stergios, Jim (January 24, 2012). Chipping away at Charter Schools, Independent blog posted on the *Boston Globe* website.

17. Chieppo and Gass, Guest Opinion, op. cit.

18. Campbell, Pamela (September 25, 2009). Politics Enters Equation for Gloucester Charter School Approval, *Metrowest Daily News*.

19. Chieppo and Gass, Guest Opinion, op. cit.

20. Staff editorial (June 27, 2014). An Affront to Freedom, *Worcester Telegram & Gazette*.

21. *Nation's Educators Honor Massachusetts Governor Deval Patrick* (July 3, 2014). National Education Association website, press release. Retrieved from www.nea.org/home/59601.htm

22. CBS4's Rick Folbaum Sits Down with Charlie Crist (September 5, 2014). *CBS Miami*.

23. Caputo, Marc A. (September 10, 2014). Wedged over Vouchers, Charlie Crist Sides with Teachers Unions Over School-Choice Pastors, *Miami Herald*.

24. Florida's School Choice Showdown (September 14, 2014). Review & Outlook, *The Wall Street Journal*.

25. Ibid.

26. Ibid.

27. Garrison, Joey (June 19, 2014), Labor Unions Question Lobbying of Tennessee Charter School Center, *The Tennessean*.

28. Ibid.

29. Banchero, Stephanie (April 8, 2014). Charter-School Fight Flares Up in Illinois, *The Wall Street Journal*.

30. Ibid.

31. Ibid.

32. Bergner, Daniel (September 3, 2014). The Battle for New York Schools: Eva Moskowitz vs. Mayor Bill de Blasio, *The New York Times*.

33. Bragg, Chris (July 25, 2014). Mulgrew Details Union's Gift to de Blasio Effort, *Crain's New York Business*.

34. Baker, Al (June 3, 2014). New York City Teachers Vote for Raise and a Nine-Year Contract, *The New York Times*.

35. Kaminski, Matthew (February 16, 2014). Eva Moskowitz: Teachers Union Enemy No. 1, *The Wall Street Journal*.

36. Resmovits, Joy (February 27, 2014). Major Charter School Chain to Lose Space under New de Blasio Plan, *Huffington Post*.

37. Kaminski, Eva Moskowitz, op. cit.

38. Thousands Rally In Support of Charter Schools In NYC (October 8, 2013), *CBS New York*.

39. Ibid.

40. Ibid.

41. Hernandez, Javier C. (March 23, 2014). Gentler Words about Charter Schools from de Blasio, *The New York Times*.

42. Ibid.

43. Fitzgerald, Sandy (March 24, 2014). De Blasio Admits to Charter School Missteps, *Newsmax*.

44. Ibid.

45. Hudson, Thousands of Charter School Supporters Protest Mayor de Blasio in New York City, op. cit.

46. *The Forgotten Fourth* (2014). Families for Excellent Schools, New York, NY. Retrieved from www. familiesforexcellentschools.org/wp-content/ uploads/2014/10/TheForgottenFourth_V4.pdf

47. Families for Excellent Schools, a grassroots organization of families of public school children, which advocates to create and improve schools, compiled these numbers in two separate reports: *The Forgotten Fourth* (2014) and *Ignition Failure: Broken Schools Threaten New York State's Revival* (2015). Retrieved from www.familiesforexcellentschools.org/wp-content/ uploads/2014/10/TheForgottenFourth_V4.pdf; and 39sf0512acpc3iz0941zlzn5.wpengine.netdna-cdn.com/ wp-content/uploads/2015/01/StatewidSchoolCrisis_ V14.pdf

Chapter 6

1. Level 3 refers to the lowest-performing 20 percent of Massachusetts's public schools. The lowest achieving and least improving Level 3 schools are candidates for classification into Level 4 or 5, the most serious levels in the state's accountability system.

2. *FAQS*, National Alliance for Public Charter Schools, op. cit.

3.   Ibid.

Chapter 7

1.   *U.S. News & World Report*, op. cit.

2.   Statistical Reports (1994). *Dropout Rates in Massachusetts Public Schools*, Massachusetts Department of Elementary & Secondary Education. Retrieved from www.doe.mass.edu/infoservices/reports/dropout/9394/dorates94un.html

3.   *2014 Graduation Rate Report (DISTRICT) for All Students, 4-Year Graduation Rate,* Massachusetts Department of Elementary and Secondary Education. Retrieved from profiles.doe.mass.edu/state_report/gradrates.aspx

4.   *2014 Accountability Report*, Massachusetts Department of Elementary and Secondary Education. Retrieved from profiles.doe.mass.edu/state_report/accountability.aspx?mode=school

5.   *MCAS Tests of Spring 2014 Percent of Students at Each Achievement Level for William N. DeBerry* (September 2014), Massachusetts Department of Elementary and Secondary Education.

Chapter 9

1.   *The Nation's Report Card: 2013 Mathematics and Reading: Grade 12 Assessment*, op. cit.

2.   Schleicher et al., *OECD PISA 2012 Results*, op. cit.

3.   Balfanz, Stop Holding Us Back, op. cit.

4.   Layton, National High School Graduation Rates at Historic High, But Disparities Still Exist, op. cit.

5. *Statement From The Education Trust on 12th Grade Reading and Mathematics Results from the 2013 National Assessment of Educational Progress.*

6. Ibid.

7. Kena et al., *The Condition of Education 2014*, op. cit.

8. Fry and Kochhar, *Wealth Inequality Has Widened along Racial, Ethnic Lines since End of Great Recession*, op. cit.

9. Cohen, Patricia (February 2, 2015). Closing Education Gap Will Lift Economy, a Study Finds, *The New York Times*. This argument was previously developed in Eric A. Hanushek, Paul E. Peterson, and Ludger Woessmann (2013), *Endangering Prosperity: A Global View of the American School*, Washington, D. C., Brookings Institution Press.

10. Ibid.

11. *Chancellor Fariña Announces Increased High School Graduation Rate for Class of 2014* (December 18, 2014). News and Speeches, NYC Department of Education.

12. Wall, Patrick (November 10, 2014). City Touts Slight Uptick in College Readiness as New School Reports Go Online, *Chalkbeat New York*.

13. *Building a GradNation: Graduation Rates in Big City School Districts with High Concentrations of Low-Income Students* (Table 6) (April 2014). GradNation, America's Promise Alliance. Retrieved from gradnation.org/resource/ building-gradnation-graduation-rates-big-city-school- districts-high-concentrations-low

14. Reardon, Education, op. cit., p. 51.

15. Fry and Kochhar, *Wealth Inequality Has Widened along Racial, Ethnic Lines since End of Great Recession*, op. cit.

16. Charles, Brian (February 22, 2014). New Haven Divided by Growing Income Disparity, *New Haven Register*.

17. Stuhlman, Adam, and Chinapen, Rachel (February 25, 2014). New Haven Schools Seek $397M Budget for 2014–15, *New Haven Register*.

18. *Fast Facts*, National Center for Education Statistics, U.S. Department of Education. Retrieved from nces.ed.gov/fastfacts/display.asp?id=16

19. Survey by the National Alliance for Public Charter Schools (June 2012), op. cit.

Acknowledgments

Thanks to the many people who made this book possible, including our families for their love and support—and in some cases scrupulous editing; the people named and unnamed in this book who generously shared ideas, stories, data, and contacts; the teachers and administrators (past and present) and students of SABIS Network schools who spoke frankly about their experiences; and the outstanding team at SABIS.

In particular, we are hugely indebted to Amy Wesley of SABIS, who kept this book on track and to a high standard. The book could not have been written without her. Our gratitude also extends to Jose Afonso, George Saad, and Raipher Pellegrino for providing valuable information, fact-checking, and editorial advice.

We owe special thanks to those people who took time out from their busy schedules to speak with us so that we could write a fair and informative book. In particular, we would like to thank city mayors Alex Morse and Domenic Sarno from Holyoke and Springfield, Massachusetts, respectively; former Massachusetts mayors Michael Albano and Bob Markel; Springfield, Massachusetts School Superintendent Daniel

Warwick; former superintendents Peter Negroni and Basan Nembirkow; William N. DeBerry principal, Stefania Raschilla; Pioneer Institute's Jim Stergios; attorney and former Massachusetts legislator Jack Brennan; former CEO of State Street Bank William Edgerly; lawyer and charter school expert Glenn Delk of Atlanta, Georgia; and last, but not least, Todd Ziebarth from the National Alliance for Public Charter Schools.

We would also like to thank a group of committed early readers (some of whom also contributed stories and ideas to the book) whose thoughtful critiques improved *Last Bell*. They include Jamsheed Ameri, Kenneth Campbell, Arthur A. Ciocca, Karen Dillon, and Jamie Gass.

Finally, this book would not exist at all if it were not for Ralph Bistany and Leila Saad, the third-generation leaders of SABIS whose commitment to a for-profit approach inspired this book and has benefitted generations of students all over the world.

Carl Bistany and Stephanie Gruner Buckley

Index